CONTENTS

GLOBETROTTER™

Travel Guide

RHODES

PAUL HARCOURT DAVIES

NEW HOLLAND

NEW
HOLLAND

★★★ Highly recommended
★★ Recommended
★ See if you can

Fifth edition published in 2006
by New Holland Publishers (UK) Ltd
London • Cape Town • Sydney • Auckland
First published in 1997
10 9 8 7 6 5 4 3 2

website: www.newhollandpublishers.com

Garfield House, 86 Edgware Road
London W2 2EA, United Kingdom

80 McKenzie Street
Cape Town 8001, South Africa

14 Aquatic Drive, Frenchs Forest,
NSW 2086, Australia

218 Lake Road, Northcote,
Auckland, New Zealand

Distributed in the USA by
The Globe Pequot Press, Connecticut

Copyright © 2006 in text: Paul Harcourt Davies
Copyright © 2006 in maps: Globetrotter Travel Maps
Copyright © 2006 in photographs: Individual
photographers as credited (right)
Copyright © 2006 New Holland Publishers (UK) Ltd

ISBN 1 84537 499 1

Although every effort has been made to ensure that
this guide is up to date and current at time of going
to print, the Publisher accepts no responsibility or
liability for any loss, injury or inconvenience
incurred by readers or travellers using this guide.

Publishing Manager (SA): Thea Grobbelaar
Publishing Manager (UK): Simon Pooley
DTP Cartographic Manager: Genené Hart
Editors: Alicha van Reenen, Thea Grobbelaar
Design and DTP: Nicole Bannister, Mark Seabrook
Cartographers: Tanja Spinola, Nicole Bannister
Updated by: Robin Gauldie
Compiler/Verifier: Elaine Fick

Picture Researchers: Shavonne Johannes, Emily Hedges
Reproduction by Resolution (Cape Town) and Hirt &
Carter (Pty) Ltd, Cape Town.
Printed and bound by Times Offset (M) Sdn. Bhd.,
Malaysia.

Keep us Current
Information in travel guides is apt to change, which is
why we regularly update our guides. We'd be grateful
to receive feedback if you've noted something we
should include in our updates. If you have new
information, please share it with us by writing to
the Publishing Manager, Globetrotter, at the office
nearest to you (addresses on this page). The most
significant contribution to each new edition will
receive a free copy of the updated guide.

Cover: The Acropolis ruins at Lindos.
Title Page: St Paul's Bay, Lindos.

Note:
In the transliteration of place names from Greek to
English spellings, various authors have tried to convey
Greek sounds in different ways. The Greek gamma is
not a simple 'g' but is more guttural or can have a 'y'
sound. Thus many different spellings are encountered.
For example, Agios, meaning 'saint' and used in church
names (e.g. Agios Georgios), can also be spelt Aghios
or Ayios. Similarly 'dh' is sometimes used to convey
the soft 'th' sound of a Greek delta – elsewhere you
might find a simple 'd'. To avoid confusion, all accents
have been omitted from the place names in this guide.

1
Introducing Rhodes

The island of **Rhodes** was claimed by the ancients to be 'more beautiful than the sun' and was sacred to the sun god, Helios. Clearly, from the vast numbers of visitors (approximately one million annually), many think that the description still pertains. Today, **Rhodes**, perhaps the wealthiest and most cosmopolitan of the Greek islands, is a year-round top international resort. The sun shines for approximately 300 days of the year on its numerous monuments, attractive towns and villages and on the bodies baking on its superb beaches. Successive waves of invaders – **Persians**, **Romans**, **Arabs**, **Knights of St John**, **Ottoman Turks** and **Italians** – valued the island for its strategic position, close both to Egypt and Asia Minor.

The tourist presence is largely concentrated in the north of the island, especially around **Rhodes town**: south of **Lindos** and **Pefkos** (**Pefki**) it is still possible to escape crowds and, outside the main tourist season, find solitude in stunning coastal and mountain scenery. **Rhodes** is an excellent base from which to begin island-hopping, being both a terminus for island ferry services and an important point of call on international routes to **Cyprus**, **Israel** and **Egypt**.

Tourist numbers begin to swell in June and subside towards the end of September – most visitors travel to Rhodes during July and August when the weather can be very hot. Naturalists and walkers prefer April and May when the flowers are in bloom, while October is a marvellous time for those who simply want warmth and peace.

TOP ATTRACTIONS

★★★ Palace of the Grand Masters: most impressive of all the Crusader buildings in old Rhodes town.
★★★ Lindos: the acropolis and superbly sited village.
★★★ Epta Piges: a lush haven fed by seven springs.
★★ Petaloudes: the cool Butterfly Valley where migrating Jersey tiger moths gather in their thousands.
★ Tsambika Beach and Monastery: crowded in summer but scenically overwhelming out of season.

Opposite: *The Platoni – a bronze stag and doe guard the entrance to the harbour.*

'...

...ourth largest of the Greek islands and the ...odecanese group of islands. It lies on a ...hwest axis in the southeastern **Aegean sea** ...ely 16km (10 miles) from the **Turkish** coast. ...stline extends for 220km (137 miles) – most of ...den, sandy beaches are found along the limestone ...es of the east whereas grey sands, shingle and pebble ...redominate on the west coast.

The island has a hilly centre with two large areas of high ground forming a mountainous spine – barren **Mt Ataviros**, 1215m (3986ft), and wooded **Mt Profitis Ilias**, 800m (2625ft). Dry river beds can quickly become raging torrents in winter, especially in the mountains, but there are no permanent rivers and only a few springs and streams – such as those at **Epta Piges** and **Petaloudes**.

The basic shape of the Mediterranean basin was established some 40 million years ago when Africa was an island separated from Europe. **Rhodes**, along with **Karpathos** and **Crete** formed part of the **Cretan Arc** – a chain of mountain peaks now partly submerged – which once linked **Asia Minor** with the **Peloponnese**.

Many Greek Islands remained forested until around 8000 years ago – the dawn of 'civilization': today Rhodes, like the other islands, is a mosaic of habitats shaped by human intervention. Nevertheless, many of the scrub-covered hillsides and poor soils, so common in the Greek world, are still botanical treasure houses. The last Ice Age which covered much of northern Europe and wiped out many species did not extend this far south, leaving a rich flora, especially the variety of bulbs.

Limited areas of plain near the coast have been exploited for citrus growing and the toil of centuries has established vineyards and orchards on hillsides.

...osite: A fertile plain ...cks the coast near ...Feraklos on the eastern side of the island.
Below: *The wooded slopes of Mt Profitis Ilias (800m; 2625ft) which is part of Rhodes' mountainous interior offer good walks.*

Seas and Shores

The **Ionian sea**, the central basin of the **Mediterranean**, is well over 3500m (11,484ft) deep in a few places. The **Aegean sea**, where Rhodes is located, is shallower by contrast and winds can create hazardous conditions making landing on rocky coasts a nightmare.

All **beaches** are public and safe for swimming, with the best of them found on the east coast. Several beaches boast a Blue Flag (for excellence), though summer crowds can over-tax sewage facilities and make water quality an issue.

Climate

The **Mediterranean** climate is characterized by mild, damp winters and hot, dry summers separated by short spring and autumn periods. **Rain** falls in the winter and early spring months between **December** and **April**.

Rhodes is sheltered by the nearby Turkish mainland and lies on the same latitude as north Africa making summers very hot and the island very dry as a consequence. The *meltémi* blows along the west coast in summer strongly enough to make

FISHING

The effects of the inflow of ocean water at the western end of the Mediterranean with a higher nutrient level, make fishing catches greater in the Ionian islands than the Aegean and high prices in Rhodes reflect this. Fishermen have to travel far towards western islands to make substantial catches of **swordfish**, **tunny**, **mullet** (red and grey), **sea bass**, **squid** and **octopus**.

RHODES	J	F	M	A	M	J	J	A	S	O	N	D
AVERAGE TEMP. °C	11	12	14	16	20	24	26	26	23	20	16	13
AVERAGE TEMP. °F	52	54	57	61	68	75	79	79	73	68	61	55
SEA TEMP. °C	13	14	15	16	19	22	24	25	24	22	18	15
SEA TEMP. °F	55	57	59	60	66	71	75	77	75	71	64	69
HOURS OF SUN DAILY	5	5	6	7	10	11	12	11	9	7	5	4
RAINFALL mm	114	73	70	43	18	8	1	0	13	73	82	110
RAINFALL in	4.5	3	3	2	1	0.5	0	0	0.5	3	3	4.5

Opposite: *For a few weeks during March and April, Rhodes bursts into bloom.* **Below:** *The temperature on Lindos Beach can climb to 40°C (100°F) in summer.*

temperatures tolerable and benefit windsurfers, without bringing the storms that can crop up elsewhere in the Aegean. Beginning as a breeze at dawn, the *meltémi* rises to a crescendo around midday and falls towards evening.

Rhodes claims more hours of **sunshine** annually than any other Mediterranean island. Between June and early September few clouds puncture the blue sky. When depressions move in from the west in late **September–October**, temperatures start to fall with occasional warm showers, but even in October air temperature can be 30°C (86°F) and the sea a warm 23°C (73°F). Most rain falls in the winter months between **December–February** and heavy storms can create turbulent streams in dry rivers. Note that although Rhodes is an international resort many hotels close in winter and air and boat timetables become restricted making trips to other islands less easy.

Spring usually arrives in early **March** but is heralded much earlier in late **January** and **February** when anemones bloom. In springtime weather can sometimes be unpredictable, though there are seldom more than a few cloudy days in succession. Walkers often choose to visit Rhodes between late **April** and early **June** when the air is clear and the summer crowds have not yet arrived.

Plant Life

Rhodes offers a number of distinct plant habitats: sand dune areas, unusual in the Greek islands, occur towards the south, and sandy soils within a few metres of the sea shore are coloured by **yellow horned poppies**, **purple sea stock**, **scarlet poppies** and, in the height of summer, **white sea lilies**. Large cultivated areas exist in Rhodes but elsewhere you'll find small, rocky fields contained within stone walls making a haven of colour with a patchwork of **white chamomile**, **yellow crown daisies**, scarlet poppies, drifts of **purple catchflies** and splashes of **blue anchusa**. Colour is added to the roadsides by displays of crown daisies mixed with poppies (which always seem redder here than anywhere else) and **scarlet turban buttercups** appear on stony hillsides.

Fields and scrubby hillsides on lime-rich soils offer a bewildering array of bulbous plants which begin to bloom with the first rains in late October. **Yellow sternbergias** (*Sternbergia lutea*) and **pink colchicums** (*Colchicum cupanii*), **cyclamen** (*Cyclamen graecum*) and a tiny, **white narcissus** (*Narcissus serotinus*) bring welcome spots of colour to parched hillsides. Yet, this is nothing

VEGETATION TYPES

Phrygana (*garigue*) – the low scented scrub of the hills – can be painful to walk through with plants such as **hedgehog spurge** (*Euphorbia acanthothamnos*) and **spiny burnet** (*Sarcopoterium spinosum*). Many of the bushes are scented and become a riot of colour in spring when the woody herbs (**oregano**, **thyme**, **sage**), and pink and white **rockroses** (*cistus*) flower. Phrygana is succeeded by the taller bushes and small trees of the **maquis** (**mastic**, **strawberry**, **myrtle** and **kermes** or **holly oak**) and then merges into open woodlands of **Aleppo pine**.

compared with the main floral explosion which occurs in spring, as early as February, with the first rush of **anemones** and continuing through May. Flower lovers will find that the Aegean islands have a distinctly 'eastern' flavour to their **bulb flora**. Rhodian specialities include an **autumn crocus** (*Colchucum macrophyllum*) and a tiny yellow-flowered **fritillary** (*Fritillaria rhodia*).

In late May and June there are fewer wildflowers in bloom but thistles such as the yellow **Spanish oyster plant** (*Scolymus hispanicus*), purple **milk thistle** (*Silybum marianum*) and blue **globe thistle** (*Spinosissimos*) bring some colour to the landscape. Rocky gullies turn pink with **oleander** (*Nerium oleander*).

Greek hillsides are dotted with the thin, dark shapes of the **funeral cypress** (*Cupressus sempervirens*), often planted around chapels and enlivened by springtime splashes of pink when the **Judas trees** (*Cercis siliquastrum*) flower.

Significant forest areas still occur: **Aleppo pine** (*Pinus brutia*) is the dominant species on lower mountains growing with **cypress** (*Cupressus sempervirens*). In summer these trees and the plants beneath produce volatile oils which are fragrant but also highly inflammable. Fires, once started, can cause appalling damage, such as in 1987 when large areas of mountain forest were badly burned.

The forests are open with trees well-spaced, allowing a rich under-storey of plants to develop – particularly of flowering shrubs such as cistus. On Mt Profitis Ilias there is an attractive white peony (*Paeonia rhodia*) found only on Rhodes.

Left: *The ubiquitous goat – provides milk and meat but at the price of overgrazing.*
Opposite: *Reinhold's orchid which is abundant on Mt Filerimos.*

Wildlife

Birdwatchers will find that the best times to visit Rhodes coincide with the spring and autumn migrations: these are never easy to predict exactly. Many **birds** make their way to and from their breeding grounds in northern Europe by navigating the Turkish coast, so large numbers of birds pass through the island.

Martins, **swifts** and **swallows** are some of the first to arrive: **wheatears**, **pipits** and **larks** (including the **shore lark** with its crest) appear in cultivated fields. Raptors such as **honey buzzards**, **harriers** and **red footed falcons** can be seen soaring high on thermals. **Lesser kestrels** breed on Rhodes with colonies near Lindos; **peregrine** can be spotted along rocky coasts near Monolithos.

MAMMALS

In the Pleistocene period, Rhodes and many other large islands were home to creatures such as the **dwarf elephant** and **pygmy hippopotamus**. The animals were trapped there after land bridges with Asia Minor were severed as the level of the Mediterranean rose.

Deer were introduced on Rhodes in antiquity. As their numbers dwindled, they were re-introduced by the Knights of St John and, following hunting to extinction during Turkish rule, again stocked by the Italians.

The most colourful arrivals are the **rollers** with their metallic-blue plumage and dipping flight and **bee eaters** which appear in large numbers in the south of the island towards Cape Prasonisi.

Around Monolithos, Kamiros Skala and Mt Ataviros there are **blue rock thrushes**, **crag martins**, **ravens** and, occasionally, **alpine swifts** and **peregrine falcons**.

From April onwards **butterflies** appear. Most obvious are the **swallowtails**, both common and scarce, and a swallowtail relative, the festoons. In mountain glades there is the **Cleopatra**: a lemon-yellow, brimstone relative with bright orange patches. **Hawkmoths** are quite common, especially the tiny whirring **hummingbird hawk** which flies by day and will even drink from the edge of a glass. **Jersey tiger moths** are found on most of the islands but in Rhodes they are responsible for the famous displays in Petaloudes (*see* p. 94). The great **peacock moth** looks like a small bat as it flies around mercury vapour lamps in Rhodes town.

Above: *The starred agama or Rhodes dragon (Agama stellio).*
Below: *The southern festoon – a spring butterfly (Zerynthia polyzena).*

You may spot a **praying mantis** or **adult cicada** on a tree branch although they are more easily heard than seen. Malaria has been eradicated but **mosquitoes** are still a pest – try locally sold repellents and plug-in machines.

There are several species of snake recorded on Rhodes but the **blunt-nose viper** (*Vipera lebetina*) is the only species dangerous to humans and is nowadays uncommon. **Lizards** seem to be everywhere, from tiny pale **geckos** on walls near lights at night to the big **Rhodes dragon** or **starred agama** (*Agama stellio*) with its distinctive large head. The **starred agama** can grow up to 30cm (12in) in length and you will often see them running across roads or up the trunk of an old olive tree to hide in cracks. Tiny green **tree frogs** (*Hyla arborea*) can be heard at night in the trees: in spring temporary ponds are alive with vocal **marsh frogs** (*Rana ridibunda*).

Conservation

Greece has just recently become active in conservation even though some of its famous sons were writing about denudation of hills and dangers of erosion over two thousand years ago. The small but dedicated membership of the **Hellenic Society for the Protection of Nature** (24 Nikis Street, Athens) has been a relentless driving force on the mainland and on the islands.

A society has also been formed on Rhodes to protect the deer which are in danger of being shot by poachers.

AT THE SEASHORE

Rhodian beaches tend not to be rich in shells – little is washed up on shore because the tidal rise and fall is small. Occasionally, after winter storms, beachcombers will find brownish, hairy balls formed from sand and the broken leaves of a marine plant, **Neptune Grass** (*Posidonia oceanica*). Visitors snorkelling close to shore will be able to spot **sea urchins** and colourful fish such as **peacock wrasses** or **scarlet soldier fish** and perhaps the occasional **octopus**.

Below: *Centuries of cultivation on Rhodes have shaped the landscape – not much truly wild remains.*

Opposite: *The Greeks excelled in their depiction of figures as on the grave stele from Kamiros.*
Below: *Ialyssos, one of the three city states created by the Dorians, perhaps in the 12th century* BC.

HISTORY IN BRIEF

Cave finds have provided evidence pointing to **Stone-Age** human activity in Rhodes – probably immigrants from Asia Minor, around 4000BC. These first Rhodians were followed by waves of **Bronze Age** settlers – Carians from Anatolia, Phoenicians from Asia Minor who established trading bases and temples and then **Minoans** from Crete who are thought to have established the first shrines at Ialyssos, Kamiros and Lindos.

Mycenaean and Dark Ages 1500–776BC

The Mycenaeans were a race from mainland Greece (the Peloponnese) who, like the Minoans, also evolved a successful palace-ruled civilization. Mycenaean influence on Rhodes was extremely important and, by 1500BC, the island had been colonized by 'Achaeans' (Homer's term for the Mycenaean followers of Agamemnon and Achilles). The Achaeans were essentially a military race who richly decorated their weapons and funeral artefacts with gold and jewels. They built a trading empire across the eastern Mediterranean and became embroiled in a ten year war against Troy which ended in 1180BC. Homer wrote that Rhodes contributed nine ships under **Tlepolemos**, son of Heracles, to aid the struggle.

The Dorians

Often regarded by historians as barbarians, the Dorians invaded from the north around 1100BC and a **Dark Age** (so-called because comparatively little is known about it) fell over much of the Greek world. Trade subsided and some islands lost the art of writing. In Rhodes, the Dorians divided the island into

three-city states (Lindos, Kamiros and Ialyssos) and in the eighth century created an association of six cities, the **Dorian Hexapolis**. This involved the city states on Rhodes, the island of Kos, together with Knidos and Halicarnassus in Asia Minor. Although these city states retained their independence, strong economic, political and religious links were established largely as a tactical response to a confederacy of Ionian cities in Asia Minor. This remarkable union prospered for four centuries and its members established wide trade links with Cyprus, Egypt, Syria and the Phoenicians of Asia Minor as well as other Greek states. Rhodes flourished and established colonies in Sicily (650BC), southern Italy, Spain and France.

Re-emergence 800BC

Greek influence began to grow again in the Mediterranean region (800BC), largely revitalized by trade links (especially with Phoenicians), and city states such as Athens and Sparta became prominent. Rhodes sided with the Persians in the Persian Wars (490–479BC) but

---

HELLENIST CALENDAR

2800–1000BC Bronze Age.
1700 Minoans establish shrines on Rhodes.
1600–1150 Mycenaeans (Achaeans) occupy Rhodes.
1000 Dorian Hexapolis established between six city states.
550 Kleobulus rules in Lindos.
490–479 Battles of Marathon and Salamis end Persian threat (Rhodes was allied with Persia).
478 Delos centre of Maritime League. Rhodes joins.
431–404 Athens crippled by Peloponnese War. Rhodes switches allegiance from Athens to Sparta.
408 Synoecisim – city states (Ialyssos, Kamiros, Lindos) unite to found City of Rhodes.
331 Alexandria founded in Egypt. Becomes important

trading partner for Rhodes.
323–180 Hellenistic Age.
305–304 Poliorketes attacks Rhodes but fails to capture it.
304–292 Chares of Lindos builds the Colossus of Rhodes.
225 Earthquake. Colossus tumbles, Rhodes city in ruins.
42BC Cassius plunders Rhodes.
AD51 St Paul visits Lindos.
155 Earthquake on Rhodes.
269 Goths attack Rhodes. Rhodes attacked by Goths.
395–1453 Byzantine Period.
653 Saracens take control of Rhodes, sell Colossus for scrap.
1082 Venetians establish trading post in Rhodes.
1204 Venetians control islands.
1261 Rhodes ruled by Genoese.

1309–1522 Rhodes becomes base for Knights of St John.
1453 Turkish conquest of Greece begins.
1522 Knights of St John defeated by Ottomans.
1523–1912 Turkish rule.
1821–27 Greek War of Independence.
1911–12 Rhodes gained by Italy under Lausanne Treaty.
1943–45 Mussolini falls, Germans occupy Rhodes.
1947 Dodecanese islands returned to Greece.
1967–1974 Colonels' Junta.
1981 PASOK Socialist government elected in Greece.
1990 PASOK defeated.
1993 & **2000** PASOK re-elected.
2002 Drachma replaced by Euro.
2004 ND ousts PASOK.

CULTURE VULTURES

Rhodes, along with Alexandria, became a centre of learning and culture to rival Athens in the third century BC. Rhodian sculptors like **Chares** of Lindos and **Pythocritus** were among the finest of their age, attracting pupils and followers from all over Greece. Many famous Romans were trained at the **School of Oratory** on Rhodes founded by **Aeschines** who (so Rhodians say) outshone his rival **Demosthenes**. Former pupil **Cassius** plundered Rhodes when the Rhodians refused to aid him in his struggle against **Octavian**.

Although the cultural explosion associated with Classical Greek civilization was centred on Athens, other islands also produced figures of equal if not longer-lasting importance: **Hippocrates** (Kos – father of medicine), **Pythagoras** (Samos – mathematician and philosopher), **Sappho** (Lesbos – poetess).

after the great Athenian-led victories at Marathon and Salamis, switched allegiance and joined the Delian League (479BC) set up by Athens with Aegean states. During the Peloponnese Wars (431–404BC), Rhodes again switched allegiance, and sided with Sparta.

Creation of Rhodes

In 408BC the three city states of **Kamiros**, **Lindos** and **Ialyssos** united to form a new capital, Rhodes City – a process known as synoecism. The cultural and economic growth which followed in the wake of its creation was remarkable, though individually the city states experienced a slow decline. The new city of Rhodes was laid out and built according to plans and principles established by **Hippodamus of Miletus**. Its five harbours were well equipped and, at its height, the city supported a population of around 100,000.

After **Alexander the Great** occupied Kos (336BC), Rhodes sided with him against Persia, showing again a political opportunism which subsequently opened lucrative trading opportunities with Egypt and Syria. In 331BC Alexander founded the city of Alexandria in Egypt using the government of Rhodes as a political model. Following Alexander's death in 323BC, the empire was divided among his generals. In 305–304BC Rhodes was attacked by **Demetrios Poliorketes** (son of Alexander's general, Antigonus, and nicknamed 'the Besieger'), for refusing to join an attack on Ptolemy, ruler of Egypt. Despite his 40,000 men and his 'state of the art'

siege machines, Poliorketes was thwarted. His abandoned machinery was sold to build an offering to the sun god Helios – the Colossus of Rhodes, fabricated by sculptor **Chares of Lindos**.

Roman Times

In 304BC Rhodes established a pact with Rome and enjoyed unrivalled success as a commercial and naval centre until the third Macedonian War from 171–168BC.

Left: *There is no record of what or who was sacrificed on this altar at Kamiros.*
Opposite: *Byzantine and Classical civilization valued Lindos for its unrivalled position.*

Rhodes' decision to side with **King Perseus of Macedonia** brought swift retaliation: Rhodes lost its territories in Asia Minor and its commercial trade was devastated when the Romans made the island of Delos a free port in 166BC. Another pact forged in 164BC made Rhodes dependent upon Rome but the final blow came in 42BC when, following the death of **Julius Caesar**, Rhodes refused to support **Cassius** in his struggle against his enemy **Octavian** (later Caesar Augustus). Both men had studied at the **School of Oratory** on Rhodes (*see* p. 16). Cassius attacked Rhodes out of revenge – inhabitants were slaughtered, buildings were destroyed and treasures (including many of the 3000 statues reputed to have graced the City of Rhodes), were carried off by Cassius to Rome. Rhodes was stripped of any influence and the city fell into a slow decline.

Christianity and After

The conversion of the populace to Christianity began in AD51 with the arrival of the **apostle Paul** at Lindos. In AD155 an earthquake caused widespread devastation from which Rhodes did not recover. The island was left as an easy target for attack by the Goths in AD269 and later by Arabs, Saracens and Turks in the centuries following the partition of the Roman Empire (AD395). Traces of Byzantine Rhodes are preserved in the early basilica churches with their mosaic floors: many of the

CHRISTIANITY COMETH

St Paul's Bay at Lindos is reputed to be the place where the saint first landed on the island in AD51.

Legend claims that Paul was approaching the island in the throes of a storm. An appeal to the Lord sent a lightning bolt which split the coastal rocks, creating a haven for the apostle to land.

The islands of the eastern Mediterranean played an essential role in early Christianity: the apostle Paul and his companion Barnabas visited the island of **Cyprus** in AD47 and made a convert in Sergius Paulus, the Governor – though not before Paul was flogged.

Above: *Influences of the Knights and Ottomans contribute to the unique mix that is old Rhodes town.*

THE KNIGHTS OF ST JOHN

In 1070 a group of Italian merchants in Amalfi founded a religious and charitable order of Benedictine Knights – the Knights of St John. The order's first patron saint was **St John the Almsgiver** of Cyprus. Members became known as the **Knights Hospitallers** through their role in protecting pilgrims and caring for the sick. Originally there were some 600 Knights drawn from noble families and ruled by a Grand Master. They were divided into eight 'inns' on the basis of 'tongues' – Auvergne, France, Provence Germany, England, Italy and the division of Spain into Aragon and Castile.

fortresses associated with the Knights were first built by the Byzantines in defence of their western outposts against pirate attack. For a time the **Saracens** took control of the island and although **Byzantine** rule was later regained, it was the Saracens who sold off the fallen Colossus for scrap in AD634.

The Age of Crusades

Lindos harbour became important to the Crusaders both for supplies and for the skill of local shipwrights in building speedy vessels. The Venetians established a trading post in 1082 and took control of trade on Rhodes; **Richard the Lionheart** brought his fleet there in 1191. After the defeat of Byzantium (1204) by the Franks, **Leon Gavalas**, the Byzantine governor of Constantinople, appointed himself ruler but was plagued by the antipathy of the Venetians. Rhodes eventually came under **Genoese** control after the island was returned to Byzantium in 1261.

In 1306 the **Knights of St John** bought Rhodes together with Kos and Leros from Vignolo, the Genoese admiral, and by 1309 had made the island their headquarters. Skilled builders, they began the fortifications and buildings in Rhodes town which are its great attraction today.

The Ottoman Turks and Italian Occupation

In 1480 the Knights managed to resist a 90-day siege by the Turks led by **Sultan Mehmet II**, 'the Conqueror'. In 1522 **Süleyman the Magnificent** brought a much larger force of about 100,000 men and, after six months, Rhodes was defeated. The remaining Knights were allowed to go to Malta. Rhodes remained under Turkish control until 1912 and throughout that time no Greek was allowed to remain within the walls of Rhodes City after nightfall. Following the Turkish-Italian war, the Lausanne Treaty of 1912 gave Italy control over Rhodes and the other Dodecanese islands – the **Isole Italiane dell' Egeo**. During this period the Italians put up many new buildings as well as rebuilding a lot of damaged structures. In 1943, following the fall of **Mussolini**, German forces invaded the island. British troops liberated Rhodes in 1945 and created a transitional Government until 1947 when, at the Paris Peace Conference, Greece regained control of the Dodecanese.

THE COLONELS

The aim of the Junta – the group of Colonels prompted by the CIA to stage a military putch in 1967 – was a moral cleansing of Greece. Dissidents were imprisoned and tortured by the secret police: many disappeared. On 17 November 1973, students at the Athens Polytechnic went on strike – the rebellion was quelled with tanks and many died. Papadopoulos, head of the secret police, was arrested. His successor, Ioannides, tried to unite the country on a wave of nationalism by assassinating Makarios and uniting Cyprus with Greece. The bid failed and the Junta fell.

Post-World War II

From 1945–49 Greece became embroiled in a bloody civil war between communist and monarchist forces – the latter, American-backed, won. On 21 April 1967, a CIA-backed *coup d' état* brought the Colonels to power. Their repressive regime ended in 1974 when they attempted to topple **Makarios III** in Cyprus in an abortive effort to incite nationalist fervour. The Turks invaded Cyprus and the island has been partitioned since. The Colonels were deposed and, since that time Greece has, once again, enjoyed democratic rule. The monarchy was formally abolished in 1975.

Below: *An Ottoman fountain – reminder of a Turkish rule of nearly four centuries (1522–1912).*

GOVERNMENT AND ECONOMY

Greek people follow politics with an avidity and awareness which surprises many visitors. Greece has enjoyed a period of relative political stability since 1974, served by a single house parliament with 300 members. Former law professor and technocrat, Kostas Simitis of PASOK (Pan Hellenic Socialist Movement), succeeded Andreas Papandreou as prime minister in 1996 following the latter's lengthy illness and subsequent death. Andreas Papandreou, Greece's octogenarian prime minister, was a wily politician and skilled economist who, in recent years had survived numerous potentially embarrassing 'U' turns on policy and election promises and more than a hint of scandal over his personal life. The omnipresent tension with Turkey casts a shadow over Greek politics both in relation to Turkey's intransigence concerning the 'Cyprus question' and its refusal to recognize Greek rights to oil beneath the Aegean sea bed.

Economy

For much of the 1990s Greece had one of the weakest European economies. Inflation was endemic and double the European average. However, the fall of the drachma relative to other currencies made Greece good value for visitors. Economic growth has improved markedly since the election of Prime Minister Kostas Simitis in 1996 (re-elected in 2000), though unemployment remains unacceptably high.

Tourism has become the major source of income in Rhodes in recent years – some two-thirds of the island's resident population are engaged in the industry in some way. Though **building** has now slowed down, hotel construction provided a great deal of

TOURISM

Rhodes began to capture the attention of the travelling public in the early 1960s. Lindos, in particular, became a favourite destination of 'famous' people – members of Pink Floyd and the astrologer Patrick Wallker bought homes there. Rhodes will long continue to be a favourite tourist destination but, in general terms, Greece is no longer top of the tourist lists. It has suffered from the financial power of the large tour operators who switch their attention at will to wherever they can make a financial killing. To counter this, Greece has set its sights on the 'quality' end of the market and the minister of Commerce is determined to energize the tourist trade.

local employment and craftsmen are working successfully in cottage industries. **Ceramics**, **leatherwork**, **wood carving** and hand-made **carpets** have found new outlets through upmarket souvenir and craft shops.

Agriculture

Rhodes has always been a fertile island and has now adopted the irrigation system pioneered in Israel permitting two harvests per year. Cooperatives make **wheat**, **winter barley** and other crops viable, although the comparatively small plains make using large machines impractical.

Exports of both **wines** from the vine growing area around Embonas and **olives** have been increasing steadily. However, income from agriculture has been decreasing as a whole.

Throughout Greece, centuries-old methods of agriculture are being abandoned rather than modernized as young people eschew the hard graft of a life on the land and make for cities and resorts. **Fishing** has declined in importance as catches have fallen due to over-fishing all around the Mediterranean.

Above: *Industrious craftsmen and women have successfully adapted their skills to the tourist trade.*
Opposite: *Though a small part of its economy, wine production on Rhodes is growing rapidly.*

The Infrastructure

On Rhodes there is a good road system between ports and main centres. Other roads away from the coast, however, can rapidly degenerate to paved (or rough) single track road. Public transport along the coasts is effected by regular bus services but inland villages are served only by a single daily bus, if at all. From June to September, the large numbers of visitors put a severe strain on water supplies and sewage handling. This poses a serious problem throughout the Greek islands because of the danger of pollution and the threat to the quality of the sea water.

> **RISKY BUSINESS**
>
> Cautionary tales abound of people seduced by a holiday into trying to run a business in Greece. If you feel like attempting the same, remember rules, regulations and laws are a minefield made for Greeks by Greeks. It can work if you have a Greek partner, preferably linked by marriage!

Right: *Fishermen in Rhodes sustain an age-old trade, often struggling to make a living in seas with depleted fish stocks.*

THE PEOPLE

Travelling for trade has been a necessity for the people of Rhodes throughout the island's history, not only between island and mainland but much further afield. Large numbers of people of Greek origin live in the USA, UK, Australia and South Africa and inevitably they become involved in commerce of some sort.

Yet wherever they end up, Rhodians retain an undying affection for their island. There are sometimes intense rivalries between islanders involving niggling village issues which go back to Classical times – usually the source of good-natured banter rather than the blood feuds associated with the Maniots in the Peloponnese.

Family Life

In general, island Greeks are extremely friendly people – their word for stranger and friend – *xenós* – is the same. Although this friendliness is still evident in the villages of Rhodes, it can be severely stretched in summer by the antics of holiday revellers. Locals are mostly tolerant, however, and mindful of the benefits brought by tourism. Greek males sometimes make a play for foreign female visitors – it's a game of point scoring among the men called *kámakia*. Some ladies welcome the attention – if it's unwanted, it pays to be polite but very firm.

Newspapers outside Greece have been quick to warn of an increase in reported rapes of female tourists – a phenomenon virtually unknown within Greek culture. But Rhodes is a very cosmopolitan island and women can enjoy a drink or a meal alone. For a foreign male to become seriously involved with a Greek girl can still create opposition, even in the most enlightened families. Greeks have a genuine love of children – as visitors with families quickly find out – and Greek children, sons especially are indulged. Serious crime is rare and Rhodians are swift to point out that much of the petty theft that exists is brought in by tourists.

Language

Greek is the official language of Rhodes and until recently existed in two forms: *dhimotikí* – the everyday language of ordinary folk – and *katharévoussa* – the formal language of officials (dispensed with, to the relief of many, by Andreas Papandreou). Modern Greek evolved from ancient Greek and utilizes the same alphabet but incorporates many words taken from the languages of various ruling powers – French, Turkish and Italian. Rhodes is so geared to international tourism that all signposts are in Latin letters rather than Greek script. Most Rhodians speak English, many speak French and a high proportion of Rhodians have worked in Germany and know the language. Many older people can still remember their Italian from pre-World War II occupation. If you are prepared to make the effort and learn a few words of Greek, then, particularly in the villages, you will find it both useful and much appreciated. Remember a 'backward nod' of the head is a Greek *ochí* meaning no.

OUT OF SEASON

Henry Miller, Lawrence Durrell and many other writers have travelled to the islands to complete a 'great work'. Larger islands such as Rhodes and Crete can cater for tourists all year round but small islands literally shut up shop during the winter months and are difficult to reach. If you make it to Rhodes out of season, however, attempt a few words of Greek: you will be welcomed as a traveller rather than tourist – Greeks are marvellous at spotting the difference.

Below: *People and places – doorways and figures make Rhodes unmistakably Greek, in spite of being an international resort.*

PRINCIPAL FESTIVALS

January 1 New Year's Day
January 6 Epiphany
March Clean Monday (or Rose Monday) held 40 days before Easter
March 25 Independence Day
April Good Friday, Easter Monday celebrated
May 1 May Day/Labour Day Flower festival in Rhodes first week in May
May 21 Panayíri – Archangel Michael in Thari Monastery
June 29 Panayíri – St Peter and St Paul in Lindos
July 20 Panayíri – Prophet Elijah on Mt Profitis Ilias
July 27 Panayíri – Agios Panteleimonas in Siana.
August 6 Transfiguration of Christ at Maritsa
August 15 Assumption of the Blessed Virgin Mary
September 8 Festival of the Birth of the Virgin Mary at Skiadi and Tsambika
September 14 Feast of the Holy Cross
October 18 Panayíri – St Luke at Afandou
October 28 Ochi Day (Greeks rejected ultimatum from Mussolini in 1940)
December 25 Christmas

Religion

Christianity was adopted in Roman times and continues today, promoted by the Greek Orthodox Church to which 98% of the population belongs. The Turks did not ban Christianity and, indeed found the Orthodox Church a convenient mechanism for collecting taxes from the populace. During Ottoman times it was the church which preserved language and Greek culture and ran clandestine schools for the young.

The **Church of Rhodes and the Dodecanese** offers its allegiance to the Patriarch of Constantinople (as in Byzantine times) and is an autonomous church headed by the Metropolitan Bishop of Rhodes. Village priests with their dramatic black hats, ankle length robes and full beards form part of everyone's image of Greece. The priest carries great respect within a community, knowing everyone and everything that is going on.

One of the most colourful times to visit villages is the **panayíri** – festival of a local saint or the name-day of a particular church or monastery and usually held in the vicinity of the establishment. Rhodians love festivals and although some have been adapted for tourists the experience is still very 'Greek'.

There is still a small Moslem population of around 2000 based in and around Rhodes town.

Greeks revere their places of worship and, whatever a visitor's views on religion, offence is avoided if they

Opposite left: *The goddess Aphrodite frozen in alabaster (90BC).*
Opposite right: *Sun god Helios, patron of Rhodes (190BC).*
Right: *Full beards and traditional garb: Orthodox priests are as much part of Greece as the landscape.*

enter modestly dressed. Convention still dictates that Greek widows wear black for years following the death of a husband or other loved one and traditionally women, from middle-age onwards, would be permanently in black as relatives died. Men are only required to wear a black armband for a year.

Myths and Legends

Tales of the Greek gods and goddesses, their rivalries, affairs and involvement with human kind have fascinated Rhodians for centuries.

In the beginning there was **Chaos**: from Chaos emerged **Gaia** (mother earth) who gave birth to a son **Uranus** (sky). The union of mother and son produced an unholy brood which included the **Titans** and the one-eyed giants, the **Cyclops**.

There are many tales of how Rhodes was founded. According to one, **Telchines**, the dog-headed sea demons with flippers for hands, were the first Rhodians. They made the sickle which **Kronos**, leader of the Titans, used to castrate his father, Uranus; they carved statues of the gods, forged **Poseidon's** trident and founded the city states of Ialyssos, Kamiros and Lindos.

Another version relates that **Alia**, sister of the Telchines, produced six sons and a daughter by the sea god Poseidon. The daughter, nymph **Rhodos**, became sole heir of Rhodes when **Zeus** destroyed the Telchines.

The tale most often cited on Rhodes involves Zeus, ruler of the Olympian gods. In order to make amends after leaving Helios out of the apportioning of the earth's territories among the gods, Zeus gave him Rhodes, which had at that time only just appeared from the sea. **Helios** married Rhodos, daughter of Poseidon, and named the island in her honour.

THE GODS – A WHO'S WHO

GREEK • ROMAN
Aphrodite • Venus
love, beauty, mother of Eros
Apollo • Apollo
poetry, music and prophecy
Ares • Mars
war, son of Zeus and Hera
Artemis • Diana
fertility, goddess of moon, famous huntress
Athene • Minerva
wisdom and war
Demeter • Ceres
harvest and agriculture
Dionysos • Bacchus
wine and fertile crops
Hephaestos • Vulcan
heavenly blacksmith
Hera • Juno
wife of Zeus
Hermes • Mercury
god of physicians, traders and thieves, messenger
Pan • Faunus
part man part goat, god of woods, flocks and shepherds
Persephone • Proserpina
queen of Underworld
Poseidon • Neptune
sea, brother of Zeus
Zeus • Jupiter
sky, Overlord of Olympos

Music

Aegean melodies have haunting cadences. The rhythms and time signatures are almost hypnotic and harken back to Classical times when the poetry of Homer and others was declaimed to the accompaniment of the *lyra* using simple five tone scales without harmonies. Ottoman, Arab and Byzantine music later developed this. Today village music is played on the *askómandra* or *tsamboúna* (bagpipes), *violí* (like a violin held on the knee), the *klaríno* (clarinet) and a *sandoúri* (hammer dulcimer).

RHODIAN POTTERY

Finds from tombs at the ancient cities of Lindos, Ialyssos and Kamiros have revealed much of what is known about Minoan and Mycenaean occupation of Rhodes. Mycenaean pottery employed designs with **vertical bands** which evolved in the 'geometric period'.

Trade with Asia Minor and Egypt influenced design and from the seventh century **animal motifs** were popular, using both real and fanciful creatures as in **Fikelloura pottery** found near Kamiros which has lotus flowers and partridges. Modern Rhodian **plates** make ready use of these designs, in addition to the colourful patterns popular in the 16th and 17th centuries under Ottoman rule.

Dance

At festivals and weddings the dancing is very different from the contrived displays: the secret is *kéfi* – the Greek equivalent of 'soul' – where the spirit really does move the dancer. In Rhodes, the best places to see traditional dance are at the village festivals or at the **Nelly Dimoglou Theatre** in Rhodes town.

The national dance, **kalamatianó**, is a 12 step *sírto* (a slow, almost shuffling dance) in which a leader improvises and the rest follow, hands joined and held at shoulder level. Zorba's dance, which is played in hotel displays of dancing for tourists, is a version of the *hasápiko* or butcher's dance.

Sports

For Greeks, the one thing which incites national passions more than politics is football. There is a large stadium in Rhodes town and during national or international matches the atmosphere is unforgettable.

For visitors the major attraction is the incredible range of water sports, always available at the larger resorts throughout the island.

Crafts and Customs

Traditional village crafts such as embroidery, lacemaking, pottery and especially ceramics are thriving on Rhodes where a ready market is found with visitors.

Rhodian plates are distinctive and customarily make use of primary colours in strong designs: plates geared to the souvenir trade draw on mythological or historical scenes. Inside a traditional Rhodian home, the walls were often decorated with plates – the more there were on display the richer the owner was supposed to be.

Art and Architecture

There are many fine surviving examples of Classical Greek sculpture and architecture on Rhodes. Byzantine religious art survives in frescoes and icons in old churches throughout the island and there are also remains of Christian basilicas with colourful mosaic floors.

The Knights showed no sentimentality towards Classical or Byzantine buildings – the former were a source of stone, the latter extended and strengthened. The result is that Rhodes has some of the finest Crusader architecture anywhere. The Turks built some mosques and converted many churches into mosques. The Italians renovated many old buildings and rebuilt parts of Rhodes town using old plans and engravings, perhaps a bit too imaginatively for some tastes. The Italians also created a fascinating hybrid Venetian-Gothic-Moorish style for public buildings and churches in Rhodes town.

MOSAICS

Mosaic floors graced the houses of wealthy Romans and also public buildings such as communal baths. The best mosaics were formed from cubes of coloured glass (*tesserae*) sometimes with gold leaf applied; others employed cubes of coloured stone. Pre-Christian mosaics depict scenes taken from tales of the Greek gods and heroes. Later compositions were laid over the earlier versions with the influence of Christianity showing up in geometric designs and floral motifs. In general, human subjects are shown full face, but animals, pagans and the wicked are depicted in profile. Originally, mosaics were kept highly polished, appearing much brighter than they do now.

Opposite: *Centuries-old designs are painted on today's ceramics by Rhodian artists.*
Left: *Characteristic black and white pebble mosaics (hochlaki) decorate a floor in Lindos.*

Food and Drink

Good Greek food is not a contradiction in terms as some people try to suggest. At best its bears favourable comparison with any Mediterranean cuisine. Wait and watch where Greeks go rather than rush to the obvious tourist establishments. In cosmopolitan Rhodes, most restaurants have learned that other Europeans like their food hot – not tepid ('better for the digestion'), as is the Greek custom.

Starters include *taramasaláta* (made with smoked cod's roe), *tzatzíki* (yoghurt with garlic, mint and cucumber), *eliés* (green or black olives), *rossikisaláta* (potato salad with mayonnaise), *yigándes* (haricot beans in tomato sauce or vinaigrette), *kolokithákia* (deep-fried courgette) served with *skordhália* (a simple garlic sauce), *mavromatiká* (black-eyed beans), *sagnáki* (fried cheese), and small pasties of cheese (*tiropitta*) or spinach (*spanachópitta*). Rhodes caters well for **vegetarians**: the idea of not eating meat through choice is accepted, though it remains totally alien to Greeks. In Greek a vegetarian is *hortofágos* (grass eater) – which says it all.

Fish tends to be expensive in Rhodes and imported – local catches have shrunk due to over-fishing. Worth trying are: *barboúnia* (grilled red mullet), *marídhes* (fried whitebait) and *xifía* (swordfish marinated in oil and lemon and grilled). *Kalamarákia* (deep-fried squid) are excellent when caught fresh; *garídhes* (shrimps or prawns) are always expensive.

Meat dishes include *keftédhes* (meatballs), *biftékia* (a sort of rissole-cum-hamburger), *souvlákia* (grilled kebabs), *arni psitó* (roast lamb) and *katsíki* (roast kid).

WHERE TO EAT

In Rhodes, fast-food outlets and international restaurants with menus in English, German and Swedish are well established. Although mainly drinking establishments, **oúzeri** also serve snacks (*mezédhes*), though the genuine article is becoming rare. **Street stands** (*girós*) serve sandwiches (*híro*) and kebabs (*souvláki*) either to take away or eat at a table. **Estiatórias** are essentially 'restaurants', usually more up-market places than the ubiquitous **tavernas**. **Psárotavernas** specialize in fish, and **Psistarías** sell spit-roast meats.

Local fruit and vegetables are excellent in season. Rhodians have a very sweet tooth: they buy cakes and pastries from a **zacharoplastía** (patisserie-cum-café) rather than as a restaurant dessert: *baklavá* is nut-filled puff pastry soaked in sugar syrup, *kataifi* is chopped walnuts and honey wrapped in shredded wheat. **Honey**, usually of the very runny kind, is a great favourite in Rhodes and often served poured over creamy fresh yoghurt. Useful lunchtime or picnic stand-by's are the larger versions of the pasties mentioned above made with filo pastry: *tiropitta* filled with minted cheese, *spanachópitta* filled with spinach and cheese or *eliópitta* filled with black olives. **Féta** is the best known Greek cheese – if buying loose, ask to try a bit since some varieties can be very salty.

Drinks

Many foreign **beers** are made in Greece under licence: they are cheaper by the bottle than canned. **Oúzo**, the aniseed based spirit, is served with iced water, which turns it milky-white. Greek **brandies** – best known is **Metáxas** – are rougher than their French counterparts but very good as the base of drinks such as **brandy sour** or **Alexander**. Numerous liqueurs are also produced in Rhodes. Rhodian **retsina** is made from the local *Athiri* grape and is a light, refreshingly crisp wine with only a hint of resin. Uniquely Rhodian is **suma**, a strong clear grape spirit.

Wine

Rhodes had a reputation in antiquity for its wines – the tradition goes back 2400 years. Modern methods of production recently introduced are yielding some wines which are well worth trying. Most vines are grown inland from the cooler west coast around **Embonas**. There are two main producers in Rhodes. **KAIR** – a cooperative started in 1924 by the Italians – has a new plant at **Koskinou** and an old plant in Rhodes, while **Emery Wines** are produced in **Embonas** from locally grown grapes – whites from *Athiri* grapes and red from the *Amorgianos* grape.

COFFEE

In Rhodes there is a choice of coffees – an Italian heritage means decent **espresso** and **cappucino** can be found in Rhodes town. '**Nescafé**' is the generic term for any kind of instant coffee in sachets which too many hotels believe must be served with tepid water. Traditional Greek coffee is a finely ground mocha, boiled in a small pot and served unfiltered in small cups. If you have a sweet tooth ask for *kafés glykós*, medium sweet is *métrios* and, for the hardened caffeine addict, the unsweetened *skétos* or *pikrós*.

Opposite: *Fast food Greek style – the kebab seller.*
Below: *A selection of Greek starters, almost a meal in themselves.*

2
Rhodes Town

Rhodes town, situated on the northern tip of the island, is without doubt one of Europe's best preserved medieval fortress towns. Although impressive at any time, it is after sunset that the old town presents an unforgettable spectacle to any visitor arriving (or returning) by boat. Spotlights pick out the massive **city walls**, **Ottoman minarets**, the **Palace of the Grand Masters** and the **three windmills** on the harbour side.

Rhodes City, the principal port, was founded in 408BC by the process of synoecism – amalgamation of the three city states, **Kamiros**, **Ialyssos** and **Lindos** – following a break of allegiance with Athens. Originally named *Damos Rodion* (City of Rhodians), it rapidly became an important trading and cultural centre famed throughout the Hellenistic world. Nowadays, Rhodes town, as it is called, has spread over the island's northern tip and is both the administrative capital of the Dodecanese Islands and its largest town. Although the current population stands at around 55,000, this is considerably less than the numbers (about 100,000) the city supported in its Classical heyday.

The town divides neatly into new and old quarters: from the old buildings and narrow streets within the town walls to the coming and going of yachts in **Mandraki harbour** or the bustling cosmopolitan attractions of the new town, Rhodes really does have something to offer everyone almost all year round.

Many hotels lie within easy reach of the town; there are fine beaches well equipped for water sports; and the range of restaurants is enough to delight any gastronome.

DON'T MISS

*** The Collachium: the Knights' quarters.
*** Archaeological Museum of Rhodes: an incredible collection of objects showing the rich history of the island.
*** Mandraki harbour: beneath the town walls.
** Monte Smith: for the stunning views and temples of ancient Rhodes.
* The Turkish Quarter: a wonderful place to wander.

Opposite: *Ottoman arches and quiet corners abound in the Old Town.*

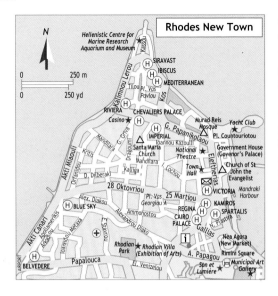

Rhodes New Town

THE OLD TOWN

The old, walled town of Rhodes with its countless small alleyways and magnificent historic buildings is a wonderful place in which to wander. In summer, the town receives some 50,000 visitors daily, although by arriving early or late in the day you can avoid crowds and oppressive heat. Restaurants with menus in English, German and Swedish reflect the countries which supply the main proportion of visitors to the island.

Walls and Gates ★★

The walls and gates to the Old Town are a magnificent legacy of the Knights Hospitallers of St John who bought the island in AD1306 and took possession in AD1309. Eight Inns of the Knights, one for each 'tongue', or nationality comprising the order (see p. 18), were built within the original Byzantine walls. In the meantime a share of the spoils from the dissolution (1312) of the Knights Templars by Philip the Fair of France and Pope Clement helped swell the coffers of the Knights Hospitallers. Later wealth of the order increased rapidly further thanks to opportunist piracy against the 'infidel'.

Quotes for the numbers of gates are confusing – originally each 'section' of the wall had its own gate, but during Ottoman times two gates facing the harbour were blocked up. The **Liberty Gate** (also known as **Pili Eleftherias** or **Freedom Gate**) was built much later, in 1924, to permit traffic access. Points of entry to the Old Town exist at Liberty Gate at the northern corner just off the Mandraki harbour and, anticlockwise around the walls, at **d'Amboise Gate**, **St George's Gate**, **St Athanasios**

CLIMATE

Summers in Rhodes town can be hot, dry and dusty. Both the nearby beaches and gardens below the Palace of the Grand Masters offer an escape. Evenings are cooler and provide relief from the days. Winters are mild with few rainy days. In spring wildflowers appear on waste ground and stone walls, bringing colour to ancient sites: days are clear and warm. Spring and autumn visitors will find that the clarity of the light brings out the best in old buildings and the warmth makes walking about pleasant.

Gate, **Koskinou** (**Agios Ioannis**) **Gate**, **St Catherine's Gate**, **Thalassini** (**Marine**) **Gate** and back to the **Arsenal Gate** just east of the Liberty Gate. You can walk around the walls on the outside at any time – but access to the walls themselves is via guided tours.

The walk begins at the massively fortified **d'Amboise Gate** (built in 1512 by Emery d'Amboise, Grand Master 1505–12). A triple-arched bridge spans the multiple ditch outside and deer graze in the moat. German Knights held the section of wall from d'Amboise gate to **St George's Gate**. Next to this gate is a bas relief showing St George killing the Dragon, and beneath is set the coat of arms of Antoine Fluvion (Grand Master 1421–37).

The Knights of Auvergne defended the next stretch as far as the **Tower of Spain** (1489) – this, like many other parts of the wall, was constructed during the tenure of Pierre d'Aubusson whose coat of arms is often seen around the walls, showing the extent of his construction work. The walls from the Tower of Spain to **St Athanasios Gate** were defended by the Spanish Knights. It was here that the conquering Süleyman entered before sealing off the gate; it was re-opened by the Italians.

The next section of wall as far as **Koskinou Gate** (**Agios Ioannis**) was guarded by English Knights, while Knights of Provence kept the following section as far as the **Tower of Italy** or **Del Caretto Tower** (Fabrizio del Caretto was Grand Master 1513–21) and Italian Knights were entrusted with the walls up to **St Catherine's Gate**.

There are marvellous views over **Emborio harbour**, which retains only three of its original 13 windmills. The Knights of Castile protected the long section of wall overlooking the harbour as far the **Arsenal Gate**. The magnificent and solid **Thalassini** (**Marine**) **Gate**, set approximately half way along the stretch, has three impressive towers.

WALL TO WALL

The Knights replaced much of the Byzantine town walls but kept the old foundations. They employed the construction skills of Italian engineers and labour of numerous slaves taken on sea raids. Each 'Inn' had responsibility for a section of the walls and construction went in phases according to the enthusiasm and ambitions of the reigning Grand Master.

The town walls stretch for some 4km (3 miles) with ramparts and turrets and have an average thickness of 12m (39ft). Their curved cross-section is deliberate – in theory it helped deflect cannon balls and projectiles. A moat 30m (98ft) wide protected the landward side.

Below: *Massive towers of Thalassini (Marine) Gate facing Emborio harbour.*

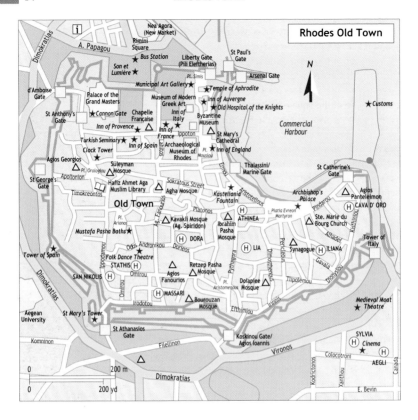

Rhodes Old Town

The Collachium ★★★

The Collachium ★★★

The Collachium housed all the buildings associated with the Knights' order and their living quarters. It is a good idea to visit either early in the morning or late in the day to avoid the stream of tourists that use Liberty Gate. Town traffic enters via this gate and leaves through the adjacent Arsenal Gate.

Just inside Liberty Gate, at Platia Simis, are the remains of a **temple of Aphrodite** dating from the 3rd century BC. Opposite the temple, the **Museum of Modern Greek Art** houses a collection of 20th-century engraving and sculpture, as well as old maps and prints; most of the paintings in its permanent collection are now

Opposite: *The Inn of Auvergne, completed by Grand Master Guy de Blanchfort (1507).*

housed in the new **Nestoridio Melathro Gallery** on Platia Haritous in the New Town (*see* p. 45).

Many of the Knights' buildings are clustered near **Platia Eleftherias** and the adjacent square, **Platia Argirokastrou**. The **Inn of Auvergne** stands on the eastern side of the square – above the portal of the inn is the coat of arms of Guy de Blanchfort, the Grand Master who completed the elegant building in 1507 (it has recently been renovated).

The **Byzantine fountain** in **Argirokastrou Square** was removed by the Italians from Arnitha where it served as a baptismal font – the carefully piled cannon balls nearby are a reminder of the Ottoman siege of 1522. In the summer months, the front of the **Old Hospital of the Knights** opposite is ablaze with bougainvillaea – Grand Master Roger de Pinsot began its construction in the latter part of the 14th century and the building served as the first hospital of the Knights until it was replaced in 1489. Both Knights and Turks subsequently used it as an arsenal. It is sometimes called **Palazzo dell' Armeria** and today is the home of the Archaeological Institute of the Dodecanese – the **Museum of Decorative Arts** is housed in the south wing. The latter has an intriguing and colourful collection of furniture, pottery, costumes, embroidery and complete rooms of old houses displaying folk art from around the Dodecanese, especially Symi. It is open Tuesday–Sunday 08:30–15:00.

THE SIEGE

Active piracy made the Knights a serious irritant to the Muslims. Rhodes was attacked in 1444 by the Sultan of Egypt and again in 1480 by Sultan Mehmet II but did not surrender. The island was besieged in 1522 by Süleyman the Magnificent. His army were held at bay for six months. After reinforcing his army, the Knights were defeated but were granted their freedom.

KNIGHTFALL

After the defeat of the Knights of St John on Rhodes by Süleyman in 1522, the surviving Knights were permitted to leave Rhodes and find a new homeland. They searched for seven years and finally found a suitable home on Malta, at a rental of one falcon per annum.

As the Knights of Malta, they withstood a siege by the entire Ottoman fleet for four months in 1565.

The English Inn of the Order ceased to exist when Henry VIII broke away from the Catholic Church in England in 1533.

Napoleon annexed Malta in 1798 and the French Revolution finally put paid to the Knights' holdings in France. In 1831 the Knights reformed as a charity based in Rome – their emblem is still used by the St John's Ambulance Brigade.

RHODES SCHOOL OF SCULPTURE

During the third and fourth centuries BC Rhodes was at the centre of developments in Classical sculpture and artists from all over the Greek world came to train there. Centuries later, great Renaissance sculptors such as Michaelangelo gained inspiration from the accuracy of portrayal of the human form by the ancient Greeks.

The **Archaeological Museum** in Rhodes has many fine examples of work from this period (see opposite) though a number were spirited elsewhere in Roman times. Among the famous Rhodian sculptors, best known are **Chares of Lindos** who created the Colossus of Rhodes in 304–292BC, **Pythocritus** who produced the Nike of Samothraki in 190BC (now in the Louvre in Paris) and **Athenodorus**, **Agesandrus** and **Polydorus**; collectively responsible for depicting the Trojan priest Lacoon and his sons being strangled by serpents (Vatican Museum).

Platia Mousiou

Literally **Museum Square**, this lies just south of **Platia Argirokastrou** and is appropriately named. The first museum you encounter is the **Byzantine Museum** in a building known as the Mitropolis. It began as the 13th-century Church of Panayia tou Kastrou (Our Lady of the Fort) and then became the late-Gothic Knights' Cathedral. In 1523, the year following the siege, the Mitropolis was the site of a Christian massacre and Rhodians later referred to it simply as the Red Church because of the blood spilled. Under Turkish rule the steeple became a minaret and the church was renamed **Enderoum**; finally it was converted back to Christian use and now houses a collection of Byzantine frescoes and paintings. Open Tuesday–Sunday 08:30–15:00.

The **Inn of England** (1483) stands across Museum Square from the Archaeological Museum, slightly separated from the other *auberges*. It was rebuilt in 1919 under Italian rule after being accidentally destroyed in 1856 (see p. 39). The narrow street beyond the inn leading off the square has some fine restaurants.

Right: *Three of the original 13 Medieval windmills still remain at Mandraki harbour.*

Archaeological Museum of Rhodes ★★★

The superb building on the west side of Museum Square rivals the Palace of the Grand Masters. Previously the **New Knights' Hospital**, it now houses the Archaeological Museum of Rhodes. (Open Tuesday–Sunday 08:30–15:00; 08:30–19:00 in summer).

Construction began in 1440 under Grand Master Jean Bonpart de Lastic whose crest, supported by two angels, stands above the entrance. Lack of funds prevented its completion until 1489 under Grand Master Pierre d'Aubusson; it was restored during Italian occupation and again after World War II. The sick and injured used to come to the hospital from all over Christian Europe. In times of war the whole of the first floor became an infirmary with capacity for over 100 canopy beds. Now the same **Infirmary Hall** is a display area for Crusader heraldic devices – tomb carvings and coats of arms. The Classical collection spans Mycenaean to late Hellenistic periods, with many objects discovered in tombs at Kamiros and Ialyssos.

Above: *The stately Palace of the Grand Masters – best known of all the Knights' many buildings.*

The best known objects in the museum are two statues of the goddess **Aphrodite**. The kneeling **Small Aphrodite** (90BC) shows the goddess combing her hair. **Venus Pudica** or **Modest Aphrodite** dates from the third century BC and was recovered from the seabed by fishermen in 1929. With her robe just falling, this statue was the inspiration for the title of Lawrence Durrell's book *Reflections on a Marine Venus*. Other treasures include a head of **Helios** the sun god (150BC), in which you can see the holes from which spikes originally emanated to form the rays of sun around his head. The famous grave stelae found at Kamiros are superbly carved reliefs – one shows **Krito** (the daughter) bidding farewell to her dying mother **Timarista** and another shows **Kalliaista**, wife of **Damokles**. There are also two stylistic figures (*kouri*) in the museum which were found on Paros and Naxos.

The Street of the Knights ★★★

The Street of the Knights (**Ippoton**) runs next to the Archaeological Museum and follows the ancient road which led from the harbour to the **Temple of Helios** where the Knights built the **Palace of the Grand Masters**.

On the right of **Ippoton Street** one finds, in order: the **Inn of Italy** (built by Fabrizio del Caretto in 1519), **Inn of France** (1492, Emery d'Amboise), **Zizim House** (named after the brother of Sultan Bayazet given asylum there), **French Chapel** and the **Inn of Provence**. The **Inn of Spain** is on the left of the street. These buildings house various institutes and galleries and most have delightful courtyard gardens.

A few columns mark the **Loggia of St John** and to the left stood the **Church of St John**, once the burial place of the Grand Masters. These, like much of the Old Town were destroyed in the Explosion of 1856 (*see* opposite).

Above: *Gate to the Inn of France, Ippoton Street.*
Opposite: *Wandering and shopping in a myriad old streets is one of the pleasures of the Old Town.*
Below: *The impressive courtyard of the Palace of the Grand Masters.*

The Palace of the Grand Masters ★★★

The Palace of the Grand Masters is apparently a reconstruction of a palace built by Helion de Villeneuve on the site of an ancient temple to the sun god, Helios. The Turks at one time used it as a prison, for stabling their horses and as a Turkish gunpowder store. It was destroyed by the

Great Gunpowder Explosion of 1856, when lightning struck a minaret and exploded the powder magazine inside. When the Italians took control of Rhodes, they reconstructed the palace as a summer home for Victor Emmanuel III (and used by Mussolini). The renovation, completed in 1939 when **Mario de Vecchi** was Italian Governor, is not to everyone's taste. Although the architects used contemporary drawings and engravings to ensure fidelity in the outer features, the interior owes little to the Knights and much to lavish Italianate design. The Roman and early Christian floor mosaics were brought from Kos by the Italians and are superb examples of mosaic art. The ground floor houses a remarkable exhibition of 2400 years of Rhodian history in various themes. Open Monday 12:30–20:00, Tuesday–Sunday 08:00–20:00.

The Turkish Quarter ★★

Although the Old Town is best known for its Medieval buildings, there is far more to be seen by those willing to wander in the old **Turkish Quarter**. The Turks moved in after the conquest of Rhodes in 1522. The town authority has woken up to the fact that, however distasteful to Greek sensibilities, the Ottoman heritage of Rhodes town is important. Many Turkish houses were destroyed under Italian rule: fortunately some houses with wood balconies remain and grants have been made available for renovation.

Sokratous Street, the Grand Bazaar and main throughfare, is a bustling place which runs west to east across the Old Town.

WHAT TO BUY

Hidden among the numerous repositories of souvenir tat on Sokratous Street, are shops selling the wares of craftsmen – **leather goods**, **gold jewellery**, **sandals**, **rugs**, **table linen**, **ceramics**, **sponges** and **umbrellas** with every designer logo you can imagine. It is worth haggling a bit if paying cash. The Ministry of Culture operates a museum shop near the Museum of Decorative Arts selling remarkably good reproductions of **Classical jewellery** and castings of **statues** and **friezes**.

CONVERSION

Following the Ottoman invasion by Süleyman the Magnificent, churches in Rhodes town and in the main towns of other islands were converted into mosques. Outside, any bell tower was rebuilt to become a minaret while inside, any human or other image was prohibited. Painted walls became plain white, statues were removed and carved tombstones set into the floors were covered with carpets. The Moslem invaders were pragmatists – they tolerated the Christian faith and the Orthodox church (useful as a means of collecting taxes away from the towns). After all, they worshipped the same God and, within their faith, Christ was another prophet.

You can start at the western end of the Turkish Quarter with the **Süleyman Mosque** by entering through St George's Gate or via d'Amboise Gate, walking directly south from the Palace of the Grand Masters (past the street artists who will sketch or paint your likeness for a price). Alternatively, start at the eastern end: enter Thalassini (Marine) Gate from Emborio harbour and walk into **Ippokratous Square** with all its fountains. Perhaps take some time to sit, as many do, and watch the world go by from the steps of the **Kastellania Palace**, formerly the stock exchange and courthouse of the Knights. And then venture forth, being prepared to take any turn south off **Sokratous Street** that takes your fancy. You will find innumerable pensions and small hotels, tiny mosques and a plethora of communal washing fountains (those who wished to enter a mosque performed a ritual washing). At night the whole place is buzzing with activity.

Süleyman the Magnificent built the **Süleyman Mosque** in 1523 to mark his conquest of Rhodes. Today's impressive pink building surmounted by a dome was built in 1828 and is open only for prayers and not to the public.

Opposite the mosque in a quiet courtyard is the **Hafiz Ahmet Aga Muslim Library** which was founded in 1794. It has a priceless collection of handwritten Korans as well as illuminated Persian manuscripts. **To Roloi**, the tall clock tower built in 1851, is impossible to miss between the mosque and town wall. There are marvellous panoramic views over the old Town from the top. Just in front of the clock tower is the **Byzantine Church of Agios Georgios**, one of a number of town churches converted to mosques (and in this case to house a religious school) by the Ottoman invaders. The conversion process was quite simple and pragmatic – walls were whitewashed, statues and icons removed, a minaret was added and fountains for ritual washing were set up around. Some of the mosques have now been converted back to Orthodox use.

A short walk along **Ippodamou Street**, running south of the Süleyman Mosque, takes you into a different world, more east than west. Here, arches span the narrow cobbled streets which separate the buildings (not an architectural nicety but a form of protection in case of earthquakes). A turning left along Archelaou Street leads into **Platia Arionos**, once the central square of the Turkish quarter. The **Mustafa Pasha Baths** off the square is a working *hamam*. It is open Tuesday 13:00–18:00, Wednesday–Friday 11:00–18:00 and Saturday 08:00–18:00. Sexes are segregated and you must bring your own soap and towel. The nearby mosque is also dedicated to **Mustafa Pasha**.

The **Folk Dance Theatre**, on Odos Andronikou (just behind the Turkish baths), holds authentic Greek dance performances on Mondays, Wednesdays and Fridays from May through to October.

Above: *Sokratous Street – busiest thoroughfare in the Old Turkish Quarter and main bazaar for shopping.*
Opposite: *Today's Süleyman Mosque stands on the site of an earlier mosque built by Süleyman the Magnificent in 1522.*

THE JEWISH COMMUNITY

For centuries the Jewish community lived in harmony with Turks and Greeks alike. Sephardic Jews fled to Rhodes in 1492 from the clutches of the Spanish Inquisition: they had doctors, merchants and various skilled craftsmen among their number and were welcomed by the Turks. Whereas all Greeks had to leave the walled city by nightfall, Jews lived alongside Turks within the walls. The community declined with the demise of the Ottoman Empire and with the start of World War II about 4000 of a population of 6000 left. In 1943, under German occupation the remaining Jews were brutally decimated: 2000 were rounded up in the Square of the Martyrs and exported to concentration camps. Less than 200 returned, and now only a handful of families remain.

The **Basilica Church of Agios Fanourios** lies just off the square, hidden by old houses. Interesting Byzantine frescoes grace the church's unusual barrel vault. On the square itself is one of the town's most intriguing buildings: the **Retzep Pasha Mosque**. The mosque's builders evidently relied heavily on materials (columns and carved stones) from earlier Crusader and Byzantine buildings. Travelling up **Fanourios Street** takes you back to the Collachium – there are some interesting shops at the lower end: tourist traps lie near the top end.

The Jewish Quarter ★★

The old Jewish Quarter lies around the **Platia Evreon Martyron** (**Square of the Martyrs**) roughly between the Thalassini (Marine) Gate and St Catherine's Gate. It is named in memory of all the Rhodian Jews rounded up and sent to concentration camps during World War II. The fountain in the square is topped by three seahorses in bronze. On the northern side of the square lies the **Archbishop's Palace** (Palati Arkiepiskopou) – once the seat of naval administration for the Knights.

Kal de Shalom Synagogue (16th century) on Dosiadou Street, just off the square, was renovated using funds provided by expatriate Rhodian Jews. The attractive Byzantine church of **Agios Panteleimon** stands just in front of St Catherine's Gate and nearby is the **Hospital of St Catherine**, founded by Italian Knights.

Right: *Agios Nikolaos fort and the Platoni are landmarks at the entrance to Mandraki harbour.*

THE NEW TOWN

Outside the walls of the Old Town, the **New Town** offers all the wallet–emptying delights (and horrors) of any cosmopolitan shopping centre. Near the harbours there's also plenty to occupy the visitor.

The Harbours

The large ferry boats and hydrofoils pull into **Emborio harbour** underneath the Medieval walls – this was the Crusader's military harbour. Commercial vessels, tankers and freighters are accommodated in adjacent **Akandia harbour** to the southeast.

For the bustle associated with a lively harbour it is hard to beat **Mandraki**. Its name means a small sheepfold or goat pen and it was created with the founding of the ancient city in 408BC. Smaller ferry boats for the islands of Symi and Kos and water taxis for Lindos berth here, along with fishing boats and 'gin–palace' yachts. On the causeway separating it from Emborio stand three Medieval windmills – originally there were 13 milling grain.

Grand Master Philibert de Naillac (1396–1421) supervized the construction of the **Agios Nikolaos fort**, built at the end of the causeway on the site of a Byzantine tower. Legend has it that the **Colossus of Rhodes** spanned the harbour here – no trace of it remains and current thinking puts its original site on the harbour side where the **General Post Office** stands today.

The harbour entrance is now guarded by the **Platoni**: Italian-crafted bronze statues of a stag and a doe each atop a column. A she-wolf stood where the doe now does – the statue was removed to the Palace of the Grand Masters.

Viewed from a boat approaching Mandraki harbour the Palace of the Grand Masters seems to sit above the cypress trees and palms of the **Municipal Gardens**. There is a nightly **Son et Lumière** held in the gardens which re-enacts the story of the Knights including their fall at the siege of Süleyman the Magnificent (the spectacle starts around 20:15 with an English performance most evenings: Greek, French, German and Swedish versions are also held each week – details from EOT).

THE COLOSSUS OF RHODES

Chares, a sculptor from Lindos, was put in charge of the construction of the Colossus. The figure took 12 years to finish and stood over 30m (98ft) high. Legend has it that the original Colossus straddled the harbour but contemporary construction techniques would not have allowed this.

The Colossus became one of the Seven Wonders of the Ancient World: in 225BC a violent earthquake toppled it so that it lay corroding until AD653 when the Saracens sold it as scrap.

Contemporary accounts note that it took 900 camels to carry away the bronze to waiting cargo vessels.

THE NEW MARKET

The cafés lining the arches which front on to Mandraki offer a harbour view (and charge for it). For breakfast, especially, the cafés inside the New Market offer much better value without crowds and exhaust fumes.

For local wines and spirits, dried herbs, nuts and olives, the small shops round the New Market periphery are marvellous. Fruit and vegetables are piled high on the stalls inside the courtyard with the fish market at the centre. Numerous stalls selling fresh *tiropittes* (cheese pastries), pizza or *souvlákia* make picnic lunches a tempting prospect.

Below: *The Palace of the Grand Masters dominates the Rhodes town skyline.*

Places of Interest ★★

Just in front of the Municipal Gardens is the dome of the **Nea Agora** – the New Market. Although Italian-built it incorporates Moorish influences in its arches, irregular heptagonal shape and courtyard. The main shopping area begins behind the New Market: in and around **Platia Kyprou** (Cyprus Square) are various banks, jewellers and up-market boutiques. Shopaholics will find plenty to occupy them along **Amerikas** and **25 Martiou** streets as well as in the warren of small streets which lead off them.

A significant proportion of Rhodes' estimated 600 bars seem to be crammed in and around streets such as **Orfanidou Street** and **Diakou Street**, located near the seafront on the western side of town.

Much of the New Town was built during Italian rule to replace the **Greek Quarter** built under Ottoman occupation. This Italianate influence is reflected in the layout of streets and especially in the design of municipal buildings in a row, along **Eleftherias Street** (Liberty Street) which forms the harbour promenade – a favourite for the evening *volta* (stroll). Here you will find the **Bank of Greece**, **General Post Office** (the Aliens office is to the rear), **Court**, **Town Hall** and the **National Theatre**.

Left: *The Municipal Gardens, site of a Son et Lumière (sound and light show) every evening during summer.*

On the opposite side of the street, separated from the harbour by gardens, stand the intriguing **Governor's Palace** and adjacent **Bishop's Palace**, demonstrating an attractive blend of styles – neo-Gothic, Venetian and Arab – by their Italian architects. Currently these buildings are used as Government House and residence of the Orthodox Archbishop of Rhodes respectively.

The original **Evangelismos Church** (Church of the Anunciation) stood next to the Palace of the Grand Masters and was also destroyed in the Great Gunpowder Explosion of 1856. The Italians used the original plans in 1925 as a basis for rebuilding it on a site opposite the General Post Office.

The **Nestoridio Melathro** (New Gallery), on Platia Haritous in the aptly named '100 Palms' district, houses Greece's most comprehensive collection of work by 20th-century Greek painters.

On Papanikolaou, close to the Elli Municipal Beach, an elegant minaret is the landmark of the **Mosque of Murad Rais**, one of Süleyman's admirals. He was killed during the seige of 1522 and is buried in the mosque's Muslim cemetery.

SYMBOL OF RHODES

According to legend, in ancient times Rhodes was reputed to be plagued by snakes. Some Greeks still wear the traditional knee-length leather boots which offered protection against snakes in the countryside.

One story has it that the Oracle at Delphi was consulted about how to get rid of the reptiles and suggested the introduction of deer to spear the snakes with their antlers.

Another version is that Rhodes City itself was infested with snakes until Forvas of Thessaly persuaded the stags to spear the serpents – the creature has been the city's emblem ever since. By the time the Italians took over, there were no wild deer left and they re-introduced them. Today deer are kept in the moat below the Liberty Gate and on Mt Profitis Ilias.

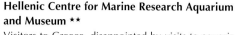

A NIGHT OUT

Rhodes at night is a magnet for hedonists: disco bunnies can throb 'till dawn in sophisticated establishments like **Le Palais** or **Amazon**. Music is everywhere – from traditional Greek (try Elli Beach for its **Bouzouki Club**) to themes for aged rockers (**1960 Bar** in Alex Diakou Street or **Sticky Fingers** pub the New Town). For formal Greek dance there is the **Nelly Dimoglou Theatre** with performances by its world-renowned company. And if a wave of nostalgia overcomes visitors with Emerald Isle connections there is always Irish music and Guinness at **Flanagan's** in the Old Town.

Hellenic Centre for Marine Research Aquarium and Museum ★★

Visitors to Greece, disappointed by visits to aquaria set up to lure tourists in resorts, will be surprised by the aquarium in Rhodes town. It is the only one in Greece built to international standards and is operated by the **Hydrobiological Institute**. By being sited underground the environment is kept cool even in high summer. Here, along a corridor displaying some 40 tanks, you can see many of the creatures visible around the coast when you are snorkelling. There are fantastically colourful fish such as **peacock wrasses**, **soldier fish**, **mullet**, both red and grey, and **octopus**. A collection of dead specimens – dried and preserved in spirit – are kept in side-rooms. The aquarium is known locally as **Enidrio** and is sited at the northern tip of the island. Open daily, summer 09:00–20:30, winter 09:00–16:30.

OUT OF TOWN

The ancient acropolis of Hellenistic Rhodes lies about 2km (1.2 miles) southwest of the main town and is known

by the decidedly un-Greek name of **Monte Smith** rather than the original **Hill of Agios Stefanos**. The hill was renamed after Admiral William Sidney Smith established a look-out there to watch for Napoleon's fleet in 1802 when Britain had allied itself with the Turks. Today, it is the place to experience the famous Rhodian sunset shown on the postcards.

The ancient city occupied a far larger area than the Medieval town, though little of it is left since it proved a wonderful source of stone for later inhabitants.

Excavations have revealed sections of road, foundations and water channels giving some idea of the extent of the ancient settlements.

Monte Smith ★★★

You can walk to Monte Smith's summit (111m; 365ft); it takes under half an hour from the d'Amboise Gate. Alternatively catch bus no 5 from Nea Agora. At the top of the hill massive segments of Doric capitals and columns are the only reminder of the forgotten grandeur of a **Temple of Zeus Polieus and Athena Polias**, once the city's most important shrine. The temple columns were brought tumbling down, so it is said, by the same earthquake which toppled the Colossus in 225BC. A few columns of a **Temple of Pythian Apollo** have been erected in an olive grove on the east side of the hill, above the third-century theatre (800 seats) and stadium, both extensively restored but with very few of the original seats.

Rodini Park ★★

The Knights once grew their medicinal herbs in Rodini Park, situated 2km (1.2 miles) south of Rhodes town on the Lindos Road. The park, a great favourite with native Rhodians and visitors alike, has been attractively set out with bridges spanning small lakes and waterways, many trees and a rose garden.

In late August the park plays host to the **Rhodes Wine Festival** but in ancient times it rang to different sounds, for here Aeschines (389–314BC) established his famous **School of Oratory** around 330BC.

Opposite: *Impressive Doric capitals and columns – remains of a temple dedicated to Zeus and Athena on Monte Smith.*
Left: *The restored Classical (3rd century BC) theatre (odeion) on Monte Smith.*

Rhodes Town at a Glance

BEST TIMES TO VISIT

In spring the sea is chilly until Jun and some rain is possible; Jul and Aug are very hot and the island is crowded with tourists. Sep–Oct are reliably hot and sunny with cooler evenings and warm seas. Many restaurants and hotels close from Nov– Apr, and it can be wet and windy from Jan–Mar. There are frequent charter flights from all over Europe from early Apr to the end of Oct.

GETTING THERE

Olympic Airlines and **Aegean Airlines** fly several times daily from Athens; Olympic also flies daily from Heraklion in Crete, and to Karpathos, Kastelorizo and Kassos several times a week. British Airways flies direct scheduled services twice weekly from London Gatwick. Up to 10 large **ferries** per week make the **Piraeus** to Rhodes trip, either travelling direct (sometimes with an extension to Limassol on **Cyprus**) or via other islands in the group: Patmos, Kalimnos, Leros, Kos, Rhodes. In summer this ferry route is extended on weekends to **Crete** (Iraklion) via Chalki, Karpathos and Kassos. Rhodes is a convenient centre for reaching smaller islands in the **Dodecanese**: 1 weekly ferry to Tilos, Nissiros, Astipalea, Kos, Kalimnos, Chalki and Karpathos. Rhodes is also well-placed for connecting with other island groups.

Cyclades: 2–3 weekly ferries to Thira, Paros and Mykonos, connections to Tinos, Andros and Rafina (on the mainland). **Aegean** Islands: 1 weekly ferry to Folegandros, Milos, Sifnos, Ikaria, Samos, Chios and Lesbos.

Hydrofoils operate from Rhodes with daily services to Kos, Patmos and Symi and connections to Kalimnos, Leros, Nissiros, Tilos, Chalki. International ferry routes link Rhodes with **Cyprus** (Limassol), **Egypt** (Alexandria), **Israel** (Haifa) and **Turkey** (Marmaris). Contact relevant port authorities for timetables.

GETTING AROUND

Good reliable **bus services** connect main towns and resorts. Shared long-haul **taxis** are common and a way of life for most islanders.

Vehicle hire – all major rental agencies (Avis, Budget, Europcar, Eurodollar and Hertz) have outlets at Rhodes airport and in Rhodes town. **Motorbikes** and **bicycles** are also for rent.

WHERE TO STAY

Rhodes gets crowded and advance booking is advisable in high season – budget hotels especially are in short supply. Lists of accommodation supplied by the Tourist Information Office in Rhodes are years out of date; more reliable is the **Rhodes Tourism Promotion Organisation**, run

by the island's hoteliers (see Useful Contacts), and the **Greek Travel Pages** website (www.gtp.net) which also has ferry and flight schedules. Rhodes has a longer tourist season than most islands, but many hotels close in winter.

LUXURY

Mansion Marco Polo, 42 Agiou Fanouriou, tel: 22410 25562, fax: 22410 25562. Gorgeous designer hotel within the walls of the Old Town.

Rodos Park Hotel, 12 Riga Fereou, tel: 22410 89700, fax: 22410 24613, www.rodospark.gr Completed in 1995, this is a comfortable, well-appointed hotel overlooking the municipal park.

Mediterranean, 35 Odos Kos, tel: 22410 24661, fax: 22410 22828. Comfortable hotel sited near the town aquarium and well placed for the beach.

MID-RANGE

Hotel San Nikolis, 61 Ippodamou, tel: 22410 34561. Comfortable rooms in a superb old house. There is a rooftop terrace for views over the Old Town and a garden.

Spartalis, Odos N Plastira, tel: 22410 24371, www.spartalis.com Comfortable and friendly, with pleasant breakfast terrace: situated opposite the quay and useful for connecting ferries.

Victoria, Odos 25 Martiou, tel: 22410 24626. A friendly family-run hotel close to

Rhodes Town at a Glance

Mandraki harbour.
Annapolis Inn, 28 Oktobriou 13, tel: 22410 26130, www.annapolisinn.gr Very comfortable apartment-hotel with pool and cocktail bar. Convenient, excellent value.
Cava d'Oro, 15 Odos Kisthiniou, tel: 22410 36980. Restored 15th-century house with inner courtyard close to the commercial harbour. All rooms have shower and toilet.

BUDGET

Mango Rooms, Doreios 3, www.mango.gr Cheap, well-appointed modern rooms on a picturesque square, with lively pub and internet café.
Iliana Hotel, 1 Gavala, tel: 22410 30251. Delightful old house in the Jewish Quarter with terrace and bar.
Hotel Stathis, Omirou 60, tel: 22410 24357. Basic, cheap, cheerful with quiet courtyard, simple rooms and low rates.
Hotel Hermes, 7 Nik. Plastira Street, near Mandraki Quay, tel: 22410 26022, fax: 22410 33160. Island hoppers can leave luggage here by arrangement.

Rhodes town is a strong contender for the best place to eat in Greece.
Alexis, 18 Odos Sokratous, Old Town, tel: 22410 29347. For the best in fish dishes both traditional and unusual.
Begleri, Cl. Pepper, tel: 22410 33353. Good location on town (Zephyros) beach –

excellent for lunch, good fish and vegetarian meals.
Café-Restaurant Meltemi, Koundourioti 8. Family-run restaurant, good seafood and salads and great location at north end of town beach, beside the Yacht Club.
Dinoris Fish Taverna, Mousiou 14A, tel: 22410 25824. Excellent fish within the walls of the Old Town.
Kamares, 15 Agios Fanourios, Old Town, tel: 22410 21337. Greek and international dishes served in traditional courtyard.
Koykos, Mandilara 20-26, tel: 22410 73022. Popular with trendy young Rhodians, this restaurant bar serves a good *pikilia* (snack plate) with each half-litre of local wine.
Nireas, 22 Platia Sofokleous, Old Town, tel: 22410 21703. Well patronized for its excellent Greek cooking.
Alatopipero Salt and Pepper, 76 M Petridi Street, New Town, tel: 22410 65494. Many *mezédhes* dishes and a wine list with a difference.

Escorted **coach** tours to Lindos, Kamiros, Ialyssos and other attractions can be booked at large hotels and tour agencies. Excursion **boats** to Lindos, Symi and Marmaris (Turkey) leave from Mandraki harbour, as do scuba dive boats. The municipal **bus** company runs six city tours, leaving from the bus stop opposite the New Market, on the Mandraki

waterfront. A '**tourist train**' also leaves from here (summer only) and goes to Monte Smith. A '**multi-ticket**' sold at the Archaeological Museum and the Grand Palace includes entry to most museums in the Old Town (but not the Roloi clock tower).

Dodekanisos Speedways, tel: 22410 70590.
Inspiration Travel, tel: 22410 24294.
Airport Information (at the Flight Desk), tel: 22410 88700.
Airport Police, tel: 22410 82882.
Automobile Association, tel: 22410 24377.
Road Emergencies, tel: 104.
National Tourist Office of Greek (NTOG), corner of Makariou and Papagon, tel: 22410 23255/23655.
Port Authority, tel: 22410 22220.
Tourist Police, Museum Square, Old Town, tel: 22410 27423.
City of Rhodes Information Centre, Son et Lumière Square, tel: 22410 23655. Open Monday–Friday 09.00–18.00, Saturday 09.00–12.00, closed Sunday.
Rhodes Tourism Promotion Organisation, Plotarchou Blessa 3, Rhodes Town, tel: 22410 74555/6, fax: 22410 74558, www.rodosisland.gr
Radio Taxis, tel: 22410 64712/64756/64734.

3
The West Coast

The fact that the beaches of the west coast are often little more than long strips of shingle has not prevented extensive coastal development for around 20km (12 miles) southwest of Rhodes town. Resorts are extremely well equipped for every conceivable water sport and have everything for a family holiday. A very wide range of hotels offers something for every pocket and in summer virtually all accommodation is block-booked for the package holiday trade.

This coast has a virtual monopoly on accommodation in the five-star and luxury class hotels which have set out to be completely self-contained. In accordance with the image of Rhodes as an all-year-round international resort, the largest hotels offer first-rate conference facilities.

South of **Theologos**, modern settlements are few and far between and instead there are several famous archaeological sites (**Ialyssos**, **Kamiros**) as well as wonderful castles below **Kamiros Skala** and at **Monolithos**.

The air on the west coast of Rhodes is seldom still and in summer the *meltémi* blows – umbrellas are available for hire as windbreaks but most are glad of any breeze which makes baking summer temperatures tolerable.

In springtime days are clear and the air is pleasantly warm: the landscape is briefly green and numerous wild flowers appear – poppies on Rhodes seem to have a redness that is vibrant. For walkers, autumn and spring are ideal times to visit and more than a few devotees have found that even at Christmas time, days are far clearer than in northern Europe.

DON'T MISS

★★★ Ancient Kamiros: remains of the old city.
★★★ Ialyssos: ancient city on top of Mt Filerimos with a restored version of an early Christian church.
★★ Monolithos: crusader fortress on a hill. Best views of the island from here.
★★ Kamiros Skala: fishing village and harbour for boats to the island of Chalki.
★ Kastellos: ruined Crusader castle near Kamiros Skala.

Opposite: *View to the coast from Monolithos castle.*

West Coast

Cape
Koumbourno

Rhodes

Kritika

Trianda Bay

Ixia

Trianda
(Ialyssos)   Tris
Filerimos (Ialyssos)

Kremasti

Paradisi   Pastida

AEGEAN   Maritsa

SEA   Petaloüdes
(Valley of the
Theologos   Butterflies)
Kalamon

Soroni   Moni
Kalopetra
Fanes

Kalavarda   Dimilia
Cape
Agios   Ancient   Agios Nikolaos
Minas   Kamiros   Fountokli
Monastery

Profitis Ilias   Apollona
Kapion   800 m
Kariona
Monastery
Mandrikon   Nanf

Koutsoútis

Kamiros   Artamitou
Skala   Monastery

Kastellos   Embonas
(Castle)   Kritinia
Makri   Agios Isidoros
Monastery
Strongili
Agios
Isidoros
Glyfada Bay

Siana

823 m

Kastrou Monolithos
(Monolithos Castle)
Cape   Monolithos
Armenistis
Cape Monolithos   Apolakkia
Bay
Strongili
Island   10 km

0

0   5 miles

Opposite: *Essential umbrellas on Kremasti beach provide relief from sun and summer breezes.*

IXIA AND THE WESTERN RESORTS ★★★

The view from the southwest-facing slopes of Monte Smith takes in the tremendous sweep of coastline which has become Rhodes' favourite package-holiday playground. But for the intervening bulk of Monte Smith, the resorts on this coast are almost suburbs of Rhodes town, only some 5km (3 miles) away. **Kritika**, closest to Rhodes town, has some small houses built by Turkish settlers from Crete.

Ixia has grown up along the busy coast road which skirts the beach before moving slightly inland at Trianda, where hotels are able to commandeer the foreshore. Unfortunately, although those hotels which are set back from the road may be relatively quiet, reaching the beach involves crossing the road, an important safety consideration for families with small children.

The lengthy but narrow beach is formed from a rather coarse, grey sand which merges into shingle and pebble but does not seem to deter the crowds in summer.

Trianda ★★★

Trianda derives its name from the summer residences that thirty of the Knights of St John had built here (*trianda* means thirty). The old name – Ialyssos – is also used and seems interchangeable with Trianda.

Exactly where Trianda begins and Ixia ends is difficult to say: in Trianda (the island's largest settlement after Rhodes town), you will find the island's biggest hotel complexes. Most are completely self-contained with every facility including huge lawns and swimming pools which obviate the need for serious sun-worshippers to compete for beach space. Several hotels boast excellent conference facilities – the **Rodos Palace**, for example, has hosted an EU summit.

Some hotels also offer direct access to the beach without the need to cross a road. At night there is no shortage of restaurants, shops and tavernas which remain open until the small hours to attract the crowds. Eating places are geared to the tourist trade – for something more Greek you will need to venture down the coast.

Kremasti ★★

In contrast to Trianda, Kremasti, just along the coast, has retained its village identity in spite of development for tourism. The fine modern church of **Panayia Kremasti** marks the entrance to the town – the building project was funded, as often happens in Greece, by funds from Greek emigrés in the USA. The faithful claim its icon of the Virgin Mary has miraculous powers: according to legend, it was found hanging in an olive tree. Kremasti literally means 'hanging', a direct reference to the icon.

Paradisi ★

Visitors to Paradisi, the next village along from Kremasti, should have a love of aircraft because the village stretches virtually parallel to the airport runway. In summer, aircraft noise is noticeable along this coast thanks to the vast number of charter flights disgorging visitors to the island. Packed summer schedules mean flights are often delayed and the village is so close that many people find it easier to wander out to get something to eat rather than suffer queues in a crowded airport.

The density of coastal development decreases as you travel west from the airport towards **Doreta beach**, near the village of **Theologos**, which (for the present) marks the end of the the main holiday coast.

SAINTS DAYS

Greek people love religious fairs (*panayíri*) and need little excuse to hold them. Apart from Easter (an important event in the Orthodox calendar), the major village *panayíri* is held in honour of the saint to whom the village church is dedicated. The Assumption of the Blessed Virgin Mary (*Panayía*) is held on August 15 throughout Greece. In Kremasti festivities last for a week beginning on the eve of the saint's day. The saint's day itself is marked with a church service and a parade through the streets. Throughout the week there are street fairs, markets, music, local costumes, dancers, abundant food and a range of events which make it one of the biggest and best in Rhodes, if not in the Dodecanese.

Below: *Our Lady of
Filerimos. The first base
for the Knights on arrival.*

FROM IALYSSOS TO ANCIENT KAMIROS

Ialyssos and ancient **Kamiros** were two of the Rhodian
city states which grew powerful after Greece's infamous
Dark Age (1000–500BC) under the Dorians. Together
with **Lindos**, the city states united to found the new **City
of Rhodes** in 408BC. Unlike Lindos, both cities declined
in importance after the foundation of Rhodes.

Ialyssos ★★★

In its heyday, ancient Ialyssos spread over the northwest
slopes of Mt Filerimos (267m; 876ft), looking over the
coast towards what is now **Kremasti**. Excavations on the
slopes from Filerimos down to the modern village resort
of Trianda and in the surrounding hills have revealed
large numbers of **Mycenaean tombs** and artefacts and
there are almost certainly many more to find.

From the coast a road, signposted from Trianda,
winds its way for some 5.5km (3½ miles) up towards the
summit of Mt Filerimos, originally the acropolis of the
ancient city. Here lie the most interesting remains: a
monastery church, foundations of a Classical temple,
traces of Phoenician paving and a Doric fountain.

The **Church of our
Lady of Filerimos** is by
far the most impressive
building on the moun-
tain. Although from the
outside it looks like a
single structure, it
includes no less than
four chapels and a
monastery, faithfully
restored during Italian
occupation. In the 5th
century AD Byzantine
monks built the first
church, a Christian
Basilica, on the remains
of the ancient acropolis:
later occupants of the

site extended the church according to their needs. The summit of Mount Filerimos became the first base for the Knights after their arrival on Rhodes – one chapel in the cluster was built by Grand Master Emery d'Amboise.

Ialyssos

Ruins of Byzantine Church

Church of our
Lady of Filerimos

Temple of Athena
Polias and Zeus
Polieus

Early
Christian Fish
Mosaic

Stairway
to Pulpit

Subterranean
Chapel

Small Chapel
d'Aubusson
Chapel

Large
Chapel

Small
Chapel

Kiosk

Early Christian
Church

Slates

Baptistry, Early
Christian
Church

Well

Cloisters

STATION OF THE CROSS
AND VIEWPOINT

N

Refectory

WC AND DORIC
FOUNTAIN

In the innermost of the chapels there is a mosaic floor with the early Christian symbol of the fish (in Greek the word for fish, *ikhthus*, forms an acronym of 'Jesus Christ, son of God, Saviour'. The cruciform baptismal font in the baptistry was built in the 5th or 6th centuries AD from stones once used in the Classical temple.

To the left of the stone stairway leading up to the church is the entrance to the subterranean Byzantine chapel of **Agios Georgios**, decorated with frescoes by the Knights of St John during the 14th and 15th centuries.

Between this chapel and the west side of the main church stand sections of columns and wall fragments which once formed the foundations of a Classical 3rd-century temple dedicated to **Athena Polias** and **Zeus Polieus**: there are also traces of a paved floor from an earlier Phoenician temple to the left of the top of the steps.

A 4th-century **Doric fountain** was exposed on the southern side of Mt Filerimos during a landslip in 1926 – one of few such fountains to have survived in Greece. The fountain had a facade of columns – water spouted from lions' heads between them. Refreshment of a different kind is now sold on Mt Filerimos, a herb liqueur – *Sette Herbe* – made to a recipe devised by Italian monks.

A signposted path leads away fom the church to a point with spectacular views down to the coast and far inland to the contrasting mountains of **Profitis Ilias** and **Ataviros** – the former with thick pine woods, the latter's summit a massive barren humpback.

FLOWERS

In springtime Mt Filerimos is full of wildflowers. Wild orchids are scattered over the hillside – most handsome being **Reinhold's Orchid** (*Ophrys reinholdii*), a bee orchid with pink sepals and deep brown lip patterned with white.

The **Violet Limodore** (*Limodorum abortivum*), is a tall purple orchid.

Above: *The harbour at Kamiros Skala – for fresh fish and the ferry to Chalki.*

A Rocky Coastline ★★

The rocky coast south of **Theologos** (Tholos) has a scattering of tavernas and small stretches of shingle beach. For much of its extent the coast is rocky but very attractive for competent swimmers who don't mind going into water from rocks (plastic sandals help). At **Soroni** there is an annual festival on 30th July at **Agios Soulas monastery**, with feasting and donkey races. For those not intending to travel further south it is worth taking the road inland to **Eleousa** and crossing the island to the east coast before making tracks for Rhodes. **Fanes** has a handful of tavernas and a strip of shingle beach. Just before **Kalavarda** it is possible to make a lengthy detour into the mountains via **Embonas** (*see* p. 98) and the vine-growing region, rather than take the coast road. Both routes lead eventually to **Monolithos**, just over halfway down the west coast. **Cape Agios Minas**, near the junction for ancient **Kamiros**, is popular with site visitors in summer, both for lunch at the tavernas and a swim to cool off beforehand.

Before the land rises again after **Kamiros Skala**, the area of coastal plain near **Mandrikon** is a sea of polythene tunnels in which melons, peppers, cucumbers, lettuce and tomatoes are grown.

Ancient Kamiros ★★★

Its setting amid hills which fall gently to the sea gives ancient Kamiros a special atmosphere: if you can plan to be there when the crowds are not, then the reward is an almost tangible sense of history.

Archaeological evidence suggests that there was a **Minoan** settlement at Kamiros – legend goes further in suggesting that **Althaimenes**, grandson of King Minos of Crete, was the founder and that a son of Hercules, **Tlepolemus**, lived here. It was rebuilt as a Hellenistic city after a violent earthquake in 226BC but abandoned and forgotten after another in AD142, covered by dust and by earth washed down the slopes. No opportunist Byzantine or Crusaders cannibalized the buildings for stone and so the layout has remained intact.

Extensive excavations have exposed the foundations of ancient Kamiros almost like a map on gently sloping terraces: the residential areas below, on the north-facing slopes, and above, a modest 'acropolis' with its religious and public buildings. Kamiros had no military significance – it was built on an exposed site and yet never had a wall. This was a working city famed for its artisans, and the houses they occupied were rather modest. Gold jewellery fashioned by the craftsmen of ancient Kamiros was well-known outside the island and, according to references in Homer, so was their pottery.

Ancient Kamiros is conveniently signposted from modern Kamiros. Open Tuesday–Sunday 08:00–19:00 in summer, 09:00–15:00 in winter.

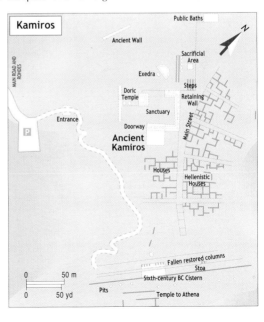

Kamiros

Public Baths

Ancient Wall

MAIN ROAD AND RHODES

Sacrificial Area

Exedra

Doric Temple

Steps

Retaining Wall

Sanctuary

Entrance

Doorway

Ancient Kamiros

Main Street

Houses

Hellenistic Houses

Fallen restored columns

Stoa

0   50 m

Sixth-century BC Cistern

0   50 yd

Pits

Temple to Athena

KASTELLOS

A ruined Crusader fortress
sits impressively on a rocky
outcrop overlooking **Kamiros
Skala** some 130m (427ft)
below. Known locally as
Kastellos (but signposted
Kastro Kritinias), it was
begun by the Knights of St
John in 1309; the tower and
walls were added later. Its
superb strategic position
enabled the Knights of St
John to command some
75km (47 miles) of coast.

Below: *The calm
vista from the Stoa
of ancient Kamiros.*

A Tour of Ancient Kamiros

The site entrance leads on to the lower or temple terrace
– with remains of a large supporting wall at its northern
boundary. Little of the **Doric temple** remains but on the
terrace's east side is a row of sacrificial altars (**Sanctuary
of the Altars**), with the largest one dedicated to sun god
Helios, the island's patron. Steps lead up to the main
thoroughfare through the residential area of the ancient
town where there are remains of **baths**, a **well-house**,
some larger **houses** with portions of columns and parts of
the **drainage system**. Near the top is an enormous **cistern**
(6th century BC) which supplied the town with water via
a system of clay pipes. But the crowning feature of
ancient Kamiros in every sense was a 3rd-century-BC
Stoa comprising two rows of Doric columns which ran
for some 200m (656ft) along the ridge above the town.
Concealed from immediate view behind the columns
was a temple dedicated to Athena Kamira – now there
are only foundations to give an idea of what might have
confronted the visitor over two millennia earlier.

Down the Coast to Monolithos
Kamiros Skala ★★

Kamiros Skala is a delightful fishing harbour some 16km (10 miles) south of ancient Kamiros and is often cited as the port from which the ancient town once exported its fine ceramic ware. However, recent excavations have shown that there was then some sort of harbour situated close to the turning for ancient Kamiros.

Kamiros Skala now has the distinction of being the only functioning fishing port on the west coast of Rhodes – its three tavernas serve the freshest fish, a fact well known to organized coach parties which make a lunchtime stop there. Otherwise, the place is remarkably peaceful. The harbour is also the departure point for ferries to the island of **Chalki** (see p. 104), which connect with the bus service between Rhodes town and Kritinia or Monolithos. The ferry acts as a 'lifeline' for the inhabitants of **Chalki** who shop and sell their wares in Rhodes and send their children to school there. There is a ruined Christian basilica in the village and on a rock wall near the port you can see a Hellenistic gravestone with an unfinished, rather worn relief.

It is worth making a detour into **Kritinia**, just a few kilometres further along the main road from Kamiros Skala. The sparkling, whitewashed houses make Kritinia look like a Cycladic village.

The tiny village church in Kritinia, **Agios Ioannis Prodhromos**, dates from the late 12th century and its frescoes span the 13th–15th centuries. The village square looks out over the coast and there are two pleasant tavernas in which to sit and relax; a folk museum lies just outside the village on the main coast road to Rhodes town.

KRITINIA OR CRETE

The first settlers in this part of the world are said to have been Minoans who named the place after their island homeland *Kriti* (**Crete**). **Althaimenes**, grandson of King Minos of Crete, is the reputed founder of Kamiros and Kritinia. Apparently, when he became homesick he used to climb Mt Ataviros because it is said that you can see all the way to Crete from the summit on a clear day.

Below: *Dazzling white Kritinia village with Mt Ataviros behind it.*

Above: *Monolithos – finest of the sites chosen by the Knights for their almost impenetrable fortifications.*

BEYOND KRITINIA

The road beyond Kritinia offers spectacular scenery with the bulk of Mt Ataviros always on the left and the land falling steeply to the sea on the right. The horizon is broken by small islands which become more hazy as the day warms. At times, perspective creates the effect of a chain of islands stretching out from the coast – **Makri**, **Strongili**, **Tragoussa** and **Alimnia** towards **Chalki**. A boat trip runs daily in summer from **Kamiros Skala** via the group of islands to Chalki and back, giving you time to stop and explore Chalki.

Just before the main road skirts **Mt Akramitis** (823m; 2700ft), the island's second highest mountain, several tracks run down to the coast. The best of them runs westward just before **Siana** down through **Lakkion**, a partly deserted village set in a wild rocky landscape. The road then continues to **Glyfada** where there is a beach of sorts, as well as fish tavernas and rooms to let in a pension. The ruined watch-tower was one of a chain built to cover the coast between the castles near Kritinia and Monolithos. Siana is worth a brief stop both for its church, **Agios Panteleimon**, built in neo-Byzantine style (1892), and for its famous produce – honey and yoghurt.

Monolithos ★★★

Mt Akramitis (823m; 2700ft) falls to the sea at Monolithos, which forms the southwestern end of Rhodes' mountainous spine. **Kastrou Monolithos** is the name of the spectacular Crusader castle which sits impregnable atop an enormous rock pinnacle, **Monopetros** ('single rock'), about 240m (787ft) high. From some angles the castle looks inaccessible – certainly the original intention – but steps lead up to it from a car park below. Of the castle, only the walls, built by Grand Master Pierre d'Aubusson (1500), now remain – together with the whitewashed church of **Agios Panteleimon**. The views from here are simply staggering. Understandably, the castle is a top tourist attraction and numerous coaches visit daily – numbers of visitors fall dramatically towards the end of the day, however, and it's then that the castle looks at its best in the warm light.

Monolithos village lies just off the main road and is quite untouched by pressure of tourists. The ascent of Mt Akramitis can also be made from Siana.

ON FOOT

Between Monolithos village and the castle, a track leads north towards the coast at Pyrgos where there is a Medieval watchtower (*pyrgos*). It forms part of a warning system which included the castle (Kastellos) situated between Kamiros Skala and Kritinia. The road is negotiable by car and after about 3km (2 miles) it divides. To the left is a detour to Pyrgos and to the right is a mountain road skirting Mt Akramitis. Take the left detour on foot.

Fourni ★★★

Fourni lies 4km (2 miles) south of Monolithos at the end of a winding road to the coast. There is a small beach of coarse sand, shingle and several caves, hidden from the beach and facing the sea. These were once used by Christians sheltering from Persians in the 7th century and later from marauding Arab sailors. Symbols of both cross and fish can be seen carved into the wall of the largest cave.

Beyond Fourni the broad sweep of **Apolakkia Bay** goes on for miles – empty beaches waiting for those who want to get away from it all.

Below: *Fourni marks the beginning of a Rhodes coastline few holidaymakers have discovered.*

The West Coast at a Glance

Although crowded in summer, resorts are well-equipped and the *meltémi* blows, making the heat more tolerable. The larger hotels cater for a year-round trade – from February to April flowers are at their best and in October the sea is still pleasantly warm.

Rhodes Diagoras Airport is situated on the west coast, 16km (10 miles) southwest of Rhodes town. Courtesy buses are available to package tourists to reach west coast resorts. For independent travellers the choice involves: **public bus services** (to Rhodes town via Ixia and Trianda), **taxi** or **Olympic Airlines bus** (tickets from Olympic Desk inside the airport) to Olympic Airlines Office, 9 Odos Ierou Lochou in Rhodes town, tel: 22410 24555.

Bus services on Rhodes are better than on most Greek islands – the **Rodos News**, a free newspaper provides exact details. Bus services operate roughly half hourly for **west coast** resorts from **Averof Street** adjacent to the New Market (Nea Agora) in Rhodes town. An hourly service operates to inland villages close to Rhodes town and up to several times daily to destinations south of **Paradisi**. There is a single bus daily from Rhodes town (departing at 14:45) for **Embonas**. **Kamiros Skala** has

an early morning bus to (and from) **Rhodes**, connecting with the ferry from **Chalki** and returning in the afternoon. A bus also leaves **Siana** and **Kritinia** in the early morning, returning in the afternoon. **Kamiros** is better served, with up to five buses daily in high summer.

The west coast station in Averof Street also serves **Koskinou**, towards the east coast of Rhodes town.

Taxis are relatively inexpensive and a widely used form of transport. Agree on a price beforehand for out of town journeys. Sharing is common practice but each person pays full rate for the part of the journey they undertake.

A **car** or **motorbike** for exploring away from the coast makes matters much easier – roads can deteriorate rapidly and most insurance policies exclude tyre and underbody damage (*see* p. 125).

Advance booking is advisable: in the main tourist season it is almost impossible to find independent accommodation on the west coast of Rhodes, which is geared to the pre-booked trade. There are many studios and self-catering apartments for hire. The Tourist Police have lists of accommodation available, or otherwise you can contact the NTOG (*see* **Useful Contacts** on p. 49). Though

Rhodes has a reputation as a year-round resort, in winter accommodation is unlikely to be completely full – at this time of year some of the hotels cater for the international conference trade.

Ixia
LUXURY
Amathus Rhodian Beach Resort, Ammochostou 29, tel 22410 21010, info@rodos-tours.com This hotel offers a mix of luxury rooms, suites and bungalows in landscaped grounds, with three restaurants, three bars, watersports and tennis court.

Ixian Grand Hotel, Ixia Beach, tel: 22410 92944, fax: 22410 94413, www.theixia grand.gr Lavishly appointed new hotel with 2577 rooms and luxury suites, three restaurants, three bars and three pools (one sea-water) as well as two children's pools.

Rodos Palace, Ixia Bay, tel: 22410 25222, fax: 22410 25350. This is a very well-equipped high-rise hotel with its own indoor and outdoor pools, gym, sauna and tennis courts. Accommodation is provided in both apartments and bungalows.

Sofitel Capsis Rhodes, Ixia, tel: 22410 25051. Huge deluxe resort complex with 680 rooms, 51 studios and apartments. An indoor as well as outdoor pool make this a good late or early-season choice. It also has a restaurant, four bars, tennis and basketball courts.

Miramare Wonderland, Ixia Bay, tel: 22410 96251, fax: 22410 95954. This is an up-market complex of superb bungalows set in mature, well-manicured gardens backing a long beach.

Cosmopolitan Hotel, Ixia Bay, tel: 22410 35373, fax: 22410 32823. Positioned across the road from the beach. Large pool and good facilities for children.

Hotel Dionysos, tel: 22410 23021, email: dionysos@hellasnet.gr This hotel is set in three buildings in well-maintained grounds. Facilities here include a cinema, two large pools and also a children's playground.

Olympic Palace, Tris Road, tel: 22410 79910, fax: 22410 30434. A huge crescent-shaped building with 1200 rooms set in lovely gardens. This hotel offers comprehensive facilities (children are well catered for) from sports to disco and entertainment.

MID-RANGE

Solemar, tel: 22410 90941. This large hotel is situated 300m from the beach and 10 minutes by bus from Rhodes town. All 102 rooms have balconies; there is a restaurant and swimming pool.

Leto, tel: 22410 23511, fax: 22410 20310. Beachfront hotel in this smart resort.

Caravel Hotel, Ixia Beach, tel: 22410 90880. This small

apartment hotel is 50 metres from the beach with 29 apartments, pool, restaurant, bar and children's playground.

Trianda

LUXURY

Filerimos Hotel, tel: 22410 92510. Fine rooms, apartments and a good taverna restaurant. There are two swimming pools; the beach is a 10-minute walk.

Hotel Golden Beach, tel: 22410 92411. Has its own private pebble beach: apartments, and hotel rooms with balconies. Well-kept gardens with very large large swimming pool plus children's pool.

Hotel Sunflower, tel: 22410 93893. Ideal for those who want good facilities yet dislike large hotels.

Kremasti

LUXURY

Armonia Apartments, tel: 22410 92077. Beautifully furnished apartments within easy reach of the sea.

MID-RANGE

Sunflower Illiotropio, just off the main west coast road, tel: 22410 93893. Friendly and comfortable 74-room hotel.

Theologos (Tholos)

LUXURY

Hotel Doreta Beach, Theologos Beach, tel: 22410 82540, fax: 22410 82446. A deservedly popular family hotel with a wide range of facilities for children and a

competent babysitting service.

MID-RANGE

Hotel Meliton, Theologos Beach, tel: 22410 41624. Well-appointed, comfortable, with pool and tennis courts.

Monolithos

BUDGET

Thomas Hotel, tel: 22416 61291. A small, very friendly hotel – each of the rooms has a kitchenette and fridge.

WHERE TO EAT

There is a cosmopolitan range of eating places all along the west coast. Some cater for 'international tastes' with burgers or smorgasbord, some offer live music accompaniment to a meal, some offer superb, traditional Greek cuisine. There are also many tavernas serving fine fish or old-style *mezédhes* washed down with excellent wine.

TOURS AND EXCURSIONS

There are daily links between **Chalki** and **Kamiros Skala** plus occasional **hydrofoils** or **boats** from Rhodes town in season. Travel agents in west coast resorts arrange trips along the coast, as well as inland to **Profitis Ilias** and to mountain villages for traditional 'Greek evenings'. In addition there are guided tours to the ancient cities of **Kamiros** and **Ialyssos**.

USEFUL CONTACTS

See Rhodes Town at a Glance.

4
The East Coast

The east coast of Rhodes is a land of contrasts. **Koskinou**, close to Rhodes town, illustrates this well – part bustling coastal resort yet, with an inland village that is still traditionally Rhodian. At **Thermes Kalitheas** is the fading glory of an Italian spa. A few miles away is the pulsating energy of **Faliraki** filled with huge hotels and vast numbers of folk intent on enjoyment of every description. **Afandou** has an 18-hole golf course and pebble beach; **Ladiko** writes large an association with the American actor Anthony Quinn who starred in a film shot there. **Epta Piges** (seven springs) is a leafy retreat, especially in spring, and the surrounding countryside a favourite with visiting naturalists. **Tsambika** is very popular and its beach, and the views down to it, are superb. A short drive further along the coast reveals **Archangelos** dominated by a fortress and dedicated to its traditions – particularly the manufacture of ceramics. Another fortress along the coast at **Feraklos** was one of the strongest built by the Knights.

Bus services are reliable between Rhodes and Lindos and the coastal road is fast for those with hire cars. There is hardly a cloud to be seen anywhere on Rhodes – island of the sun god Helios – for the whole of the summer, but the lack of *meltémi* wind along the east coast makes it noticeably hotter than the west coast. In spring, the hills and scrub flower briefly, the air is clear and area looks is at its best. Out of season there is little difficulty finding some accommodation along this coast. In summer book in advance or spend time trying to find rooms in hill villages.

DON'T MISS

★★★ **Epta Piges:** an Italian-made lake fed by seven springs – a lush haven.
★★★ **Tsambika Monastery and Bay:** some of the most spectacular coastal views.
★★★ **Faliraki:** resort for dedicated pleasure seekers.
★★ **Archangelos:** Crusader castle and traditional village crafts – especially ceramics.
★ **Feraklos:** the strongest fortress the Crusaders built.

Opposite: *Faliraki is dedicated to holiday pleasure.*

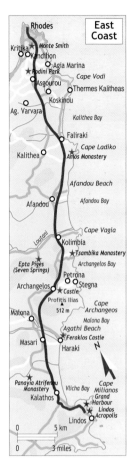

FROM AGIA MARINA TO KOLIMBIA
Agia Marina ★

The coast from **Agia Marina** to Koskinou is barely separable from Rhodes town: the bay is the location of a popular Blue Flag beach and home of numerous hotels.

Koskinou ★★

Just inland, on a steep rise, lies the village of Koskinou which in Ottoman times was a village inhabited purely by Turks. **Asgourou,** a suburb of Rhodes on the road to Koskinou, still has a small Moslem population and a mosque (once the **Church of Agios Ioannis**).

Koskinou is one of the prettiest villages in Rhodes and a good place to see traditional Rhodian houses dating from the 17th and 18th centuries. The houses have brightly painted doors and flower-filled courtyards with intricate cobbled mosaics of black and white pebbles (*hochláki*). A road from the village leads to the coast 2.5 km (1.6 miles) away where there are hotels and tavernas.

Thermes Kalitheas ★★

When the Italians decided to restore the spa at Thermes Kalitheas during the 1920s they built a distinctly Moorish pavilion with pink marble pillars, set in lush gardens. Although its splendour is faded, the spa

still attracts visitors in considerable numbers. In ancient times this spa was famed for its hot mineral springs – it was recommended by **Hippocrates**, 'father of modern medicine', for its powers in relieving arthritic joints. Thermes Kalitheas has a small beach which is served by regular buses from Rhodes and can get very crowded.

Opposite: *Faded splendour – Moorish influence and Italian style at the resort spa of Thermes Kalitheas.*
Right: *Quaint Koskinou village maintains a tradition of brightly painted doorways and windows.*

Faliraki ★★★

Faliraki rivals Ixia as the favourite package resort on Rhodes. There are numerous hotels including vast self-contained complexes and a shopping mall at Faliraki Bay North. The resort beach is long and sweeping with a gentle slope, grey sands and a Blue Flag awarded for excellence. **Watersports** enthusiasts are well served with every kind of water activity available, from parascending, water-skiing and jet skiing to windsurfing and pedaloes. The 'longest water slide in Greece' is sited at **Aqua Adventure** in the Hotel Pelagos gardens. Faliraki has an aquarium-cum-vivarium at the **Faliraki Snake House**. Open daily 11:00–23:00.

Numbers thin out slightly towards the far end of the bay where the island's only **official nudist beach** is situated. Beach amenities (umbrellas, showers and cabins) at Faliraki are generally good: there's mini-golf, go-karting, bungee jumping, and a plethora of eating places. Note, however, that it is also home to crowds and incessant disco music, that omnipresent ingredient in any 'paradise' for the 18–30 set.

BENEATH THE WAVES

A wide variety of colourful fish, sea urchins and the occasional octopus can be spotted around the rocky coastal areas. Divers should note that scuba diving is very carefully controlled because of the chance of finding valuable antiquities which can be spirited out of the country (and have been in the past). In Rhodes, diving is only permitted through two centres which offer courses from beginners to advanced: **Waterhoppers Diving School**, tel: 22410 38146 and **DMC** (Dive Med College), tel: 22410 61115. Both are well established and DMC organizes **wreck searches** and **sea bed surveys**.

Cape Ladiko marks the southern end of Faliraki. It is more often known by its local name – **Anthony Quinn Beach** – because the villagers made a gift of the beach to the actor after he filmed the Guns of Navarone off the coast just to the north of Ladiko bay.

Above: *Popular but not crowded – the sand and shingle beach at Kolimbia.*

WITCH'S BREW

Around ruins and along paths look out for the heavily-veined leaves of the **mandrake** (*Mandragora officinarum*), which form rosettes on the ground.

The flowers are bright violet at the centre and have poisonous yellow and red tomato-like fruit. Mandrake has long been used as a medicinal plant and an essential constituent of witches' brews (gathered at midnight). The taproot is supposed to resemble a human torso and the ancients believed that when pulled from the ground it emitted a curdling shriek and the person pulling died. To avoid this a dog was tied to the plant and made to pull – posterity does not record the dog's fate.

Afandou ★★

Afandou village is hidden (*afantos* means invisible) in a dip just inland from the coast, with a dramatic backdrop of mountains. Nowadays, it is known for having the island's only 18-hole **golf course** and for its superb, sweeping pebble beach with crystal clear waters. The village (population approximately 1500) is also famous for its **apricots** and for **carpet weaving** (the principal activity of many of the villagers). The village retains traditional features such as its *kafeneíon* and tavernas which are used by locals. One of the few official **campsites** on Rhodes is situated between Afandou and Faliraki (the other is at Lardos). There are no big hotels to dominate the beach but plenty of holiday flats and studios for rent and some very good fish tavernas for evening relaxation.

Kolimbia ★★

The attractive sand and shingle beach at Kolimbia, 6km (4 miles) south of Afandou, is approached along an avenue of eucalyptus trees lining the roadside. Just off this road there are remains of a 6th century Christian basilica with mosaics, on the way to the beach. Kolimbia is a popular resort, but certainly not on the Faliraki scale (although more hotels are being built) and there are good water sports facilities. A left fork off the eucalyptus avenue leads to a small cove to the north of the main beach where there are fishing boats and a taverna.

EPTA PIGES AND SURROUNDS
Epta Piges ★★★

The name Epta Piges literally means 'seven springs', a reference to the seven streams which feed this small artificial lake and waterfall. It was built by the Italians, who dammed the wooded valley 4km (2.5 miles) inland from Kolimbia. In summer on this dry Mediterranean island verdant Epta Piges becomes one of the most popular tourist spots – an oasis of greenery.

There is a pleasant woodland walk to the site from the turn-off signposted for Epta Piges, or you can drive to the café in the woods. The lake is reached by a path over the hill or a tunnel beneath it. The tunnel is 186m (610ft) long, damp and dark and thus a passage only for those who don't suffer from claustrophobia. It is slippery after winter rains and human traffic can create passing problems during the hot summer.

Below: *A cool retreat – one of the forest streams at Epta Piges – seven springs.*

There are peacocks in the valley but naturalists have long known that an even greater attraction is the number of rare, wild **orchids** growing locally. The scrubby hills just after the turning for Epta Piges are full of orchids that imitate insects in shape, colour or scent to attract them for pollination. Note **King Ferdinand's** orchid (*Ophrys regis-ferdinandii*) which is hardly flattering to royalty since it resembles a tiny bluebottle fly. There are also **pink butterfly** orchids (*Orchis papilonacea*). Keep an eye out for a **Violet Limodore** (*Limodorum abortivum*) which grows among the pine needles in the valley.

Above: *From Tsambika Monastery, the glory of the bay below is obvious.*

Tsambika Monastery and Bay ★★★

Back on the coastal road, just south of Kolimbia, is **Mt Tsambika** (326m; 1070ft) with its monastery – a tiny white-painted Byzantine church dedicated to the Virgin Mary and containing an 11th-century icon. If determination and modern medicine fails to produce a pregnancy, then a pilgrimage to **Tsambika Monastery** to pray to the Virgin Mary on September 8 is claimed to be able to do the trick. Local lore claims that children whose birth was aided in this way used to be called Tsambika (girls) or Tsambikos (boys): a very common Rhodian name!

The church is reached by a steep path from the car park below. At the top visitors can catch their breath and drink in the superb views – arguably the walk provides the finest vista on the island, stretching down to the nearby coast and Tsambika Bay. This superb bay is especially popular during the main holiday season of July and August when it can get very busy.

Archangelos ★★★

This large and prosperous village is situated 7km (4 miles) south of Kolimbia. Surrounded by citrus groves, it is famous for its **fruit** production and **village crafts** – pottery, traditional footwear and hand-woven carpets are made here. The name comes from the village churches of the **Archangel Michael** and the **Archangel Gabriel** – the former has the distinctive tiered bell tower (the 'wedding cake' campanile) found in the islands of the Dodecanese.

Many traditional aspects of village life are preserved in Archangelos, from Rhodian village houses with brightly painted doors and walls to local speech which preserves an old dialect and traditional songs. In the narrow streets of the old quarter of the village you can wander and see the traditional 'above-knee-high' boots being made. These hide boots once offered villagers essential protection against snakes; they now make a popular but pricey souvenir.

Archangelos castle, built in 1467 under the instigation of Grand Master Orsini, is now little more than a set of massive walls. It served as one of twelve fortresses protecting the coasts against pirate raids and from it you get good views of the village, the bell tower and citrus groves down to the sea.

Stegna and the Coast ★★

Surprisingly, Stegna which lies only 4km (2.5 miles) east of Archangelos has remained quite unspoiled as a **fishing village**. For those who enjoy coastal walks, Stegna makes a pleasant base for a few nights – there are comfortable pensions and some very good tavernas.

By walking along the coast either north or south from here, you can experience some of Rhodes' finest coastal scenery, where tiny sandy coves puncture the limestone cliffs of the coast. If walking in summer it is wise do so in the early morning or towards the end of the day because midday and afternoon **temperatures** of 40°C (104°F) and above are often the norm. A supply of suncream, a protective hat and a water bottle are essential.

COASTAL WALKS

The coastal paths running north and south from **Stegna** are marked by bright red dots painted on rocks. The path north to **Tsambika Bay** runs along the coast and then swings inland and up and over a rocky ridge. The view of Tsambika Bay from the top is electrifying and the descent to the bay takes you down an enormous dune slope. It is impossible to resist the temptation to swim here and, when cool, contemplate the ascent of **Mt Tsambika** at the far end of the beach. The route south from **Stegna** to **Agathi** and **Haraki** (1½–2 hours) follows the clifftops past **Mt Profitis Ilias**. Views towards Feraklos castle and all the little bays before it are breathtaking.

Below: Villagers in Archangelos maintain proud traditions in crafts, songs and a local dialect.

SOUTH FROM FERAKLOS
Feraklos ★★

The huge, ruined citadel of **Feraklos** is an imposing
sight from afar: it was once one of the best fortified of
the fortresses of the Knights of St John. Before the
Knights arrived from Cyprus, Rhodes had been taken
over by Muslim pirates who used the Byzantine fortress
as a stronghold. The Knights expelled the pirates,
improved the fortifications and used Feraklos as a
prison. In this fortress they were able to resist the forces
of Süleyman and held out under siege for some time
after Rhodes town fell (*see* p. 19).

After a climb from the track below there is little to
see at the top except walls outside and the bushes
inside. But from the top the views are superb along
Haraki bay to the south and **Agathi beach** to the north,
making the climb well worthwhile.

A track leads down from Feraklos castle to Agathi
beach which, though relatively short on facilities,
boasts superb golden sands and is good for swimming.
Development for a hotel complex is underway and

Opposite: *Women in
traditional dress are a
familiar sight in the local
community of Istrios.*
Below: *The ruined
citadel of Feraklos domi-
nates the bay below it.*

across the beach there is the diminutive **Church of Agia Agathi** built into a cave.

Haraki **

A number of small fisherman's houses reveal that Haraki was originally a fishing village. Since then, tourist development has taken it some way from that, converting it into a 'choice' resort with most accommodation in apartments, studios and pensions.

Haraki can be reached from the main road to **Lindos**, or by walking along the stunning coastal route from **Stegna** via **Agathi** or **Feraklos** (*see* box on p. 71). In the village you will find an attractive esplanade, free of traffic, backing the pebble crescent which forms the beach. From Haraki's excellent fish tavernas you get the bonus of views across the bay of Lindos.

Further along the Coast

As the bay continues in a southerly direction towards Lindos some larger hotels begin to appear at **Kalathos** and just down the coast at **Vlicha Bay**. At Kalathos there is a tiny whitewashed Byzantine church and a shingle beach which has been 'improved' by the addition of more sand. It is worth noting, however, that the beach at Vlicha is better.

Just south of Kalathos there is a choice of direction. You can either head left towards **Lindos** (for a postcard view of its fortress-capped citadel as you round the corner) or turn right and inland towards **Lardos**. The resort of Lardos is popular with the package trade but the village lying in a valley off the main coast road is quite unspoiled – if Lindos gets too busy then Lardos has a very pleasant square in which to sit with a drink. The village also possesses a number of small family-run hotels and pensions.

LINES OF DEFENCE

The castles built by the Knights have stood the test of time. Often they were built upon earlier Byzantine fortifications – both sets of builders made ample use of stone from earlier Classical sites. The Knights set up a defensive chain on Rhodes: the seven major castles are at **Kritinia**, **Archangelos**, **Asklipio**, **Feraklos**, **Lindos**, **Monolithos** and **Rhodes town**. Many watchtowers (*pyrgos*) were also built. Castles were constructed on neighbouring islands as a system of outer defences: **Chalki**, **Kalimnos**, **Kos**, **Tilos**, **Leros**, **Nissiros** and **Symi**. The Knights brought in skilled craftsmen from southern Europe schooled in the latest architectural and engineering techniques, and their piratical acts introduced a supply of slave labour.

The East Coast at a Glance

BEST TIMES TO VISIT

From Jun–Sep east coast resorts are full of pleasure-seeking visitors: safe swimming makes the resorts ideal for families. In spring and autumn the dramatic coast of Tsambika to Lindos is great for walking; flowers offer a spring bonus.

GETTING THERE

Rhodes Diagoras Airport is situated on the west coast 16km (10 miles) southwest of Rhodes town. Tourists on package holidays are transported to their resorts via courtesy buses. Independent travellers can use taxis, the public bus services or the **Olympic Airlines** bus (tickets from Olympic Desk inside the airport) to Rhodes town and the east coast bus station.

GETTING AROUND

There are two bus stations in Rhodes town, situated close together near the Nea Agora (New Market). See *Rodos News*, the free newspaper, for exact details of timetables. The East Side bus station for east coast resorts and villages is in Platia Rimini. Buses run at least hourly and also serve destinations just inland of the east coast. All Lindos buses stop at Faliraki, Afandou and Archangelos and some travel through Malona and Massari. **Koskinou**, on the eastern side, is served from the west coast station on Averof Street. **Taxis** are relatively inexpensive and therefore a widely used

form of transport. Agree on a price beforehand for out of town journeys. Sharing is common practice but each person pays full rate for the part of the journey they undertake. **Cars**, **motorbikes** and **bicycles** are available for hire through most of the hotels, who will contact the agents, or from outlets in Faliraki. Remember – the roads can deteriorate very rapidly and most insurance policies exclude tyre and underbody damage (*see* p. 125).

WHERE TO STAY

The accommodation in most of the east coast resorts is generally block-booked by major European package operators in summer. It may just be possible to find rooms to let in some of the village houses inland in the far south, and the Tourist Police also have lists of rooms for rent. Out of season accommodation is readily available although many of the smaller hotels tend to close during the winter months.

Afandou
LUXURY
Afandou Beach, tel: 22410 51586. The largest hotel in Afandou with 90 beds. It is well situated for easy access to the mixed sand/shingle beach.
Irene Palace, Afandou Bay, tel: 22410 51614. Comfortable family-run hotel; rooms have private terraces. There are large gardens, a swimming pool and

good childrens' facilites including babysitting.
Lydia Maris, Afandou Beach, tel: 22410 56294/41, fax: 22410 56424.
The swimming pool provides the central feature of this attractive holiday complex.
Kolymbia Beach Hotel, tel: 22410 56247, fax: 22410 56225. Spacious, low-rise hotel set in lawns running down to a pebbly beach.

MID-RANGE
Golden Days, tel: 22410 86900. A modest family-run hotel just outside Afandou village and away from the coastal bustle.

Archangelos
MID-RANGE
Karyatides, tel: 22440 22965. A small, well appointed hotel about 1km (0.6 miles) from the town centre; there is a swimming pool and bar selling Greek snacks.
Anthi Sun, (Ilios tis Anthis), tel: 22440 22619. A comfortable, modern hotel set in large, well-maintained gardens.

Stegna
BUDGET
Antonis, tel: 22440 22280. A modest and friendly family-run pension of seven apartments, close to the beach.
Faliraki
Most accommodation is pre-booked by tour companies.

The East Coast at a Glance

LUXURY
Esperos Village, 6.5km
(4 miles) northeast of Faliraki,
tel: 22410 86046. A large
self-contained complex in
vast gardens. Three swim-
ming pools and a well-
equipped children's play-
ground: the whole complex
dominates Faliraki beach.
Esperos Palace, 6.5km (4
miles) northeast of Faliraki,
tel: 22410 84300. Built in
Cycladic style, set in the
same gardens as the Esperides
beach and linked with the
latter by a bridge. All rooms
are air conditioned and
have balconies, many with
sea views.
Faliraki Beach Hotel,
tel: 22410 85301. Situated
just 5 minutes' walk from
Faliraki resort in its own
grounds fronting the beach.
The restaurant has its own
taverna and there are
dozens more in the
town nearby.
Hotel Rodos Beach, Kalitheas
Bay, 5km (3 miles) northeast
of Faliraki, tel: 22410
85412. Rooms in hotel and
bungalows. The beach with
waterskiing and windsurfing
is a short walk through the
hotel gardens.

MID-RANGE
Mousses Hotel, tel: 22410
85303. A small, friendly
establishment a short
distance from the beach
offering a contrast to the
huge hotels.

BUDGET
Hotel Dimitra, tel: 22410
85309. Conveniently situated
in town, a comfortable
family-run hotel with 73
beds. Very basic and simple
but good value for money.

Kalithea
LUXURY
Castello di Rodi, tel: 22410
64856, fax: 22410 64812.
Well situated for access to the
thermal baths (2km; 1 mile).
It has its own sauna, gardens
and swimming pool.

MID-RANGE
Kalithea, tel: 22410 62498.
A small hotel with 15
rooms – clean and friendly.

Kolimbia
MID-RANGE
Kolimbia Bay, tel: 22410
56268. A friendly, very comfortable hotel of modest size.
Mistral Hotel, tel: 22410
56346. Good quality three-star
resort hotel with a large
lagoon-style pool, watersports
and 115 rooms with balcony,
facing the sea or the pool.
Lutania Beach Hotel, tel:
22410 57344. This four-star
hotel complex opens onto the
beach, with a large pool, tennis
courts and watersports. It is
only three kilometres from the
Afandou golf course.

Koskinou
LUXURY
Aldemar Palace Royal Mare,
tel: 22410 66060, fax: 22410

66066, www.aldemarhotels.
com Fronted by a bay, it
offers watersports as well as
restaurants and night club.

WHERE TO EAT

Tavernas, bars, and fast food
joints sit cheek by jowl on
the beach road. Most offer
'international' dishes to suit
their changing clientele. There
are also many good restaurants
serving Greek cooking and lots
of traditional dishes. Check
the menus and price lists
and, if possible, eat where the
locals eat for the best food.

TOURS AND EXCURSIONS

All hotels advertise half and
full day excursions all over
the island (including courtesy
transport). Traditional 'Greek
evenings' with folk dancing
have also become popular in
mountain villages such as
Psinthos and **Embonas**.
Resorts and hotels have
numerous gift shops where
items range from the tacky
to beautiful examples of
traditional crafts including
carved olive wood and
jewellery. For gifts with a
Rhodian flavour it is worth
visiting Archangelos, the
island's main centre for
pottery and hand-woven
carpets. Visitors are more
than welcome to visit the
factories.

USEFUL CONTACTS

See p. 49, Rhodes Town at a
Glance, for information.

5
Lindos and the Far South

Dazzling white houses climbing the slopes of a fortress-topped hill at the end of a sweeping bay make Lindos a spell-binding destination. Lying only 56km (35 miles) on good coast roads from Rhodes town, Lindos has become the favourite tourist destination after Rhodes town. Traffic does not penetrate far into the village, which is a maze of narrow streets full of small shops, bars, restaurants and throngs of visitors. Out of season Lindos is marvellous, the locals become far more friendly and the prices tend to fall sharply.

The bay is safe, sandy and the waters crystal clear – ideal for families with children.

Lindos was settled by Minoans and a natural harbour led to it becoming one of three important cities on the island with **Ialyssos** and **Kamiros** (see p. 54). Lindos grew to be a successful trade centre and established outposts throughout the Classical world. The **acropolis** was fortified by the **Knights of St John** and now the ruins of the ancient city lie within massive walls accessible by climb or on donkey-back.

Wealthy mariners built the **Captains' Houses** which date from the 17th century. The **Bay of St Paul** below the acropolis is where the apostle is said to have landed during a storm in AD51.

At 45ºC (113ºF) and above in summer, Lindos is reputed to be one of the **hottest places** on the island, both in temperature and as a measure of its nightlife. It is also famous for its **Easter celebrations** when the climate is pleasantly warm and the verges full of flowers.

DON'T MISS

*** Acropolis: crusader fortress and Classical temple high above the bay of Lindos.
*** Cape Prasonisi: the wild, unspoiled, sandy tip.
** The Captains' Houses, Lindos: step back to the days of wealthy merchant captains of the 18th century.
** Agios Georgios Chostos: the oldest church on Rhodes with amazing frescoes.
* Plimiri: a long, sweeping bay backed by dunes.

Opposite: *St Paul's Bay, almost completely ringed by rocks.*

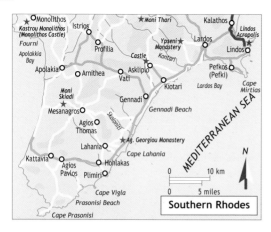

Southern Rhodes

LINDOS

In antiquity, the prosperity of Lindos depended on the sea. A superb natural harbour – now silted up – ensured its evolution as a trading centre, and ship-yards produced superb vessels which were in much demand. Lindians also founded colonies in Sicily and southern Italy.

Kleobulus, one of the 'Seven Sages' of ancient Greece, was the widely respected ruler of Lindos for some 40 years in the 6th century BC. During his reign Lindos (which had long surpassed the other city states of Ialyssos and Kamiros) became extremely wealthy and politically important in the Classical world. A stone **Temple of Athena Lindia** was built on the acropolis by Kleobulus on a site where, since the 10th century BC, there had been wooden shrine. This had contained a statue of the goddess and just below it was the sacred grove dedicated to Athena.

Following synoecism in 408BC, when the three city states united to establish Rhodes City, Lindos lost a little of its political importance but its fame as a place of pilgrimage and commercial strength lasted into Roman times. In 342BC the **Temple of Athena Lindia** burned down destroying the statue of Athena. A new temple was built and equipped with a new statue of the goddess. The wealth of votive offering is described in the **Temple Chronicles** (see p. 80) found at Lindos in 1904. The Byzantines later built walls around the acropolis and a fortress within, which became a refuge for the inhabitants during the centuries when the coasts were ravaged by Arab pirates.

The fortifications were strengthened by the Knights of St John who began building over the ancient city around the bay – later, the Ottoman Turks established a garrison on the acropolis and built houses below (17th century).

CRUSADERS – HEROES OR VILLAINS?

Tales of Robin Hood with references to Good King Richard I and deprecating comments of the infidel are examples of a propanganda war begun by Crusaders. In such fables the Crusaders are cast as heroes saving Christendom from the threat of Satan's forces on earth – the Muslim infidel.

Slowly, truth of a very different kind has emerged. The Muslims under Saladin were a cultured, creative people who revered poetry and literature and valued knowledge. They were making scientific advances at a time when Christian countries had long forgotten things the Greeks had discovered. Conveniently, accounts of Crusaders dismembering live victims, flaying, disembowelling and carrying out acts of cannibalism were quickly repressed...

Lindos Acropolis ★★★

Countless feet of inhabitants and visitors alike have polished the steps leading up to the acropolis. The climb is not arduous but you can pay for a long-suffering donkey 'taxi' to take the strain. Alongside the path you pass Lindian women selling traditional tablecloths and lace spread out on the rocks – embroidery has been a Lindian tradition since the time of Alexander the Great.

Within the acropolis – below the steep flight of steps up to the fort – is the famous Hellenistic rock carving called the **Exedra of Lindos**, which depicts the stern of a military vessel known as a *trireme*. The platform (*exedra*) is thought to have formed the base for a bronze statue of **Aghesandros of Lindos** fashioned by sculptor **Pythocritus**, creator of the **Nike of Samothraki** (190BC) which is now displayed in the Louvre in Paris (*see p. 36*).

The entrance to the fort leads though the gateway into a vaulted hall, once part of the **Governor's Palace**. The hall is now used as a museum. Above a window in the **Commander's Quarters** are the coats of arms of two Grand Masters associated with the building of the fort: Pierre d' Aubusson (1476–1503) and Antoine de Fluvian (1421–37).

On the first of a series of four terraces, after leaving the hall, is part of a 13th-century Byzantine church dedicated to **St John**. Just to the east of the church stands another stone *exedra* – this one with its statue intact (Pamphilias, Athenian priest of the 3rd century BC). The nearby foundations are probably Roman and belong to the 'whispering temple', built in a commanding position 120m (400ft) above the sea.

THE FIRST LINDIANS

The strategic advantages of the acropolis were obvious to the first **Neolithic settlers** (2000BC) and to the **Minoans** and **Mycenaeans** who followed them. The real flowering of Lindos as a city state began under **Dorian** rule in the 10th century BC. In this period it traded with other city states in the Aegean as well as with the Phoenician, Egyptian, Cypriot and Syrian merchants. It also established its own system of coinage and a system of maritime law so effective that it was later adopted by Augustus and peristed into Byzantine times.

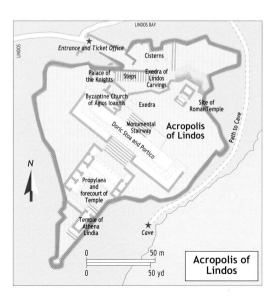

Acropolis of Lindos

Above: *Lindos – a National Historic Landmark – still maintains its charm.*

A **stoa** (colonnade) comprising 42 columns was added around 200BC – about 20 still stand. All the columns stood backed by a wall except for the eight in front of the ornamental stairs rising to the **propylaea**. All sides of the **Temple of Athena Lindia** beyond were visible from the sea below. For a current timetable of opening hours, contact the National Tourist Organization/EOT (*see* p. 122).

Lindos Village ★★★

Through the 1960s and early 70s Lindos came to represent an island idyll as artists, writers and musicians, often famous, bought property and settled there.

Lindos village has a permanent population of about 1600, in contrast to the ancient city state which supported approximately 17,000 inhabitants. Most of the ancient city foundations now lie hidden beneath the town and are likely to remain so since the whole village has been declared a **National Historic Landmark.**

It makes sense to park just outside Lindos and walk down into the village. Tourist buses go down to the square to disgorge their passengers: most visitors then make their way directly up to the acropolis and don't venture more than a few streets from the square. The narrow cobbled streets form a labyrinthine complex often canopied by vines. Many of the houses have been converted into tourist accommodation with rooms built around a central courtyard. Bags and luggage are delivered on motorised carts.

Church of the Assumption ★★
Just off the central square lies the domed **Church of the Assumption of Our Lady**, built in the 14th century and then restored by Grand Master Pierre d'Aubusson in 1490. The late Byzantine frescoes (painted by Gregory of Symi) date from around 1779; there was further restoration of the church under Italian occupation in 1927. The church floor is a mosaic of black and white pebbles (*hochláki*). One of the frescoes depicts the figure of **St Francis of Assisi** painted with a donkey's head, a fine example of the pagan sense of irreverence often found in Byzantine paintings.

There are other tiny churches scattered around the village – **Agios Georgios Chostos**, the oldest church on Rhodes, is built below ground and some of the frescoes date from the iconoclastic era (8th–9th century AD).

Lindos thrived as a centre for trade during the 15th and 17th centuries. Merchant sea captains grew wealthy and built the loveliest of all Lindian houses: the *archondika* or **Captains' Houses**. Some of the houses are available for rental and others are open to visitors. The most opulently decorated house, the **Papkonstandis Mansion**, is now the **Lindos Museum** and another, the **Kashines House**, displays a traditional **Lindian bridal dress** (*sperveri*).

Below: *The distinctive bell tower of Agios Georgios Chostos, the oldest of the island churches.*

Above: *The Captains' Houses of Lindos – a reminder of a wealthy maritime past.*

The Captains' Houses

The Captains' Houses show a unique blending of different styles. Lintels are usually carved with a cross (rather similar to the emblem of the Knights) enclosed within a cabled pattern. Arches are a blend of the Gothic and Moorish and framed by the same cable pattern. The doorway (*pylonias*) leads into a courtyard with a pebble mosaic characteristic of the Dodecanese. Rooms lead off the courtyard – the largest (*sala*) was used both for entertaining and sleeping, with beds on raised carved platforms and brightly coloured bed covers (*sperberi*). Walls are adorned with decorated Lindian plates. The so-called Captain's room, characteristic of the larger houses, usually sits above the gateway looking out to sea and to the street.

Houses in neo-Classical style, complete with columns, were built towards the end of the 19th century by wealthy Lindians, usually returning expatriates anxious to demonstrate their new-found fortune to those who had stayed at home.

OUT OF TOWN
The Tomb of Kleobulus ★

From the northern end of Lindos Bay there is a path out to the headland which offers excellent views back over the acropolis and town. At the end is a massive cylindrical tomb built from square stone slabs dating from approximately the 1st century BC. Known as the **Tomb of Kleobulus** (although pre-dating the king) it was probably the tomb of a well-to-do family and one of the many tombs discovered in Lindos. In Medieval times it was converted into a Christian chapel and subsequently dedicated to **Saint Emilianos**.

Theatre ★★

The theatre which served ancient Lindos (4th century BC) looks out over the sea on the southwestern slope of the acropolis. It had twenty-six rows of seats arranged in two sections and could accommodate some 2000 people – there are also traces of a temple to Apollo on the same site and nearby foundations of a gymnasium.

Voukoupion ★

No blood could be spilled within the confines of the Temple of Athena – goddess of purity – thus bullocks were sacrificed at the Voukoupion, a small sanctuary on the northern slope of the acropolis.

Lindos Beach ★★★

The appeal of Lindos beach is obvious even if in high summer it is difficult to see the sand between the umbrellas from a distance. The sheltered bay with its gently shelving beach, golden sands and crystal clear water is ideal for families and extremely popular in summer with **swimmers**, **windsurfers** and **waterskiers** (with plenty of instruction available). Towards its northern end, Lindos bay merges with popular **Pallas beach** and a rocky headland favoured by nudists.

ICONS AND SYMBOLISM

The creative energies of the greatest artists of the Byzantine era were devoted to a celebration of the Christian religion in icons and frescoes. Examples can be found in many of the old churches on the island. Figures on icons are painted in highly stylized fashion, trying to capture the spiritual side in a way worshippers recognized. The iconoclasts (AD726–843) considered any portrayal of sacred figures to be blasphemous.

Frescoes have their styles and conventions and many mix elements of Biblical scenes with contemporary influences – figures are shown in medieval rather than Biblical dress. Agios Georgios (8th–9th centuries), the underground chapel in Lindos, has fishes and ships as part of the ornamentation.

Left: *The sweep of Lindos Bay to the village and the acropolis beyond – one of the most photographed views in Rhodes.*

Right: *The 11th-century Monastery of Metamorfossi (Kimisis Theotokou), famed for its remarkable frescoes.*

St Paul's Bay ★★

This delightful, secluded bay is almost completely ringed with rocks. It can be reached from the coast road or, better still, by a walk through the labyrinthine alleyways of Lindos village. Here, in AD51, St Paul is said to have sheltered from a storm on his way to Palestine.

Neighbouring Beaches ★

Most tourist development has taken place either side of the Lindos peninsula and has gradually encroached on the village. To the north, the busy resort of **Kalathos** is situated just before the junction for **Lindos/Gennadi**. It lies at the southern end of **Vlicha Bay** which has a long shingle and sand beach.

By taking a bus to Vlicha Bay and walking back towards Lindos you reach some marvellous panoramic views of the town and citadel, particularly pleasant in the evening when the main road is quieter. There is a also a track leading inland for approximately 800m (2625ft) after the Lindos/Gennadi junction which sweeps around and into Lindos via a rocky valley.

To the south, **Pefkos** (Pefki) has seen a rush of development in recent years, although not in any organized fashion. It is an ideal escape from busy Lindos, with a narrow sandy beach fringed by pine trees only a few minutes' walk from a car park. The coast road towards **Lardos** allows access to other sandy stretches of the coast around **Lardos Bay** – a favourite resort with the package trade.

SOUTHWARDS FROM LINDOS

The coast road will take you well south of Lindos in an hour and a half, making it possible to comfortably explore the far south of Rhodes from Rhodes town as a base. Travelling south is easier down the east coast since the roads are less twisting than on the west side of the island.

Cultivation rather than tourism is the mainstay of the region and a paucity of petrol stations makes it essential to keep a careful eye on the petrol gauge.

Asklipio ★★

Asklipio lies directly inland from Kiotari and is reputed to be the birthplace of the Greek god of healing – **Asklepios** (*Aesculapius*), son of Apollo. In ancient times the village was a centre of healing to which islanders would have made pilgrimages and where the followers of Asklepios exerted a dual function as priests and healers of the sick. A ruined castle dominates the village but most visitors come to see its superb church, the **Monastery of Metamorfossi**, or **Kimisis Theotokou**, a domed 11th-century Byzantine basilica with 15th-century frescoes depicting Old Testament scenes. Next to the church is a small village museum set up by the villagers themselves. Bread is still made in the early morning in communal wood-fired ovens (*foúrnos*). And there is no food in the Hellenic world to compare with warm village bread – what the gods of Olympos surely meant by *ambrosia*. At Easter the women of the village bake traditional breads and biscuits in the outdoor ovens.

Below: *Asklipio – an ancient village baking the best bread on Rhodes.*

Above: *The crescent of Plimiri Bay – dune-backed for those who want to escape the crowds.*
Opposite: *The stunning scarlet turban buttercup (Ranunculus asiaticus) dots the landscape during the spring months.*

Kiotari ★★

Kiotari sits on the coast on the site of the original Asklipio: inhabitants were forced inland during the Ottoman period by the continual threat of pirate raids. Many villagers from Asklipio now have beach huts at Kiotari beach which stretches for miles along the coast.

Gennadi ★★

The old coast road, although rutted and full of potholes, provides access to a series of quiet coves down towards Gennadi beach and further south west to Plimiri. Gennadi, just inland from the coast and beach, is still a quiet town by day, but at night its tavernas and supermarkets spring to life when holiday-makers return from a hard day on the popular shingle beach of the same name.

St George and Lahania

At **St George**, just southwest of Gennadi, some luxury hotels have sprung up in recent years and the resort is now great for water sports. Further down the coast, there is a very pretty sheltered cove at **Glistra** and as the road swings inland you arrive at **Lahania.** Once almost deserted, Lahania has been rescued by foreigners who have bought up and tastefully renovated village houses.

Plimiri ★★★

This area of the coast has a superb 'get away from it all' beach forming a great crescent shape backed by dunes which are never crowded, even in summer. A marina has recently been built and there is an old church just behind the extremely good fish taverna, constructed on the site of a Christian basilica using bits of the original.

THE FAR SOUTH
Kattavia ★

Kattavia, the southernmost village on Rhodes, is a useful watering hole with cafés, tavernas and the only petrol station around for miles. Visitors tend to congregate in the main square, yet, in the streets away from the centre, Kattavia is a delightfully sleepy Greek village with brightly painted houses and flower-filled gardens.

Cape Prasonisi ★★★

Literally 'green island', Cape Prasonisi forms the **southernmost tip** of Rhodes: the headland is separated from the coast joined only by a narrow sandy isthmus. The swell on the Aegean side of the spit to the west makes it a windsurfers' paradise and in summer large numbers of enthusiasts make their way here in hired jeeps along the rough road from Kattavia. Tavernas provide sustenance and many visitors camp here (unofficially). On the eastern side of the headland the sea is much calmer although in rough winter seas the isthmus disappears altogether.

In springtime **Cape Prasonisi** is an idyllic place where it is possible to be the only one on the spectacular sandy beach. The surrounding countryside is full of flowers – wild anemones, scarlet turban buttercups and orchids (see p. 55). A few weeks later the scrub seems to burst into flower with bushes of rockroses covered in white or pink blooms and sometimes beneath them, growing on the roots, the yellow and red parasitic plant Cytinus (*Cytinus hypocistus*).

WINDSURFING

Windsurfing for beginners and novices is available at all resorts on Rhodes. **Lindos** and **Lardos**, with their sheltered beaches, are good for beginners, but experienced windsurfers and kite-boarders head for **Prasonisi**, where the bay to the west of the sandy isthmus offers the best windsurfing conditions on Rhodes. Elsewhere on the west coast, **Apolakkia Bay** is also good for windsurfing. Every resort beach on the resort strip from **Ixia** to **Agia Triada**, as well as **Faliraki**, has its quota of independent outfits offering boards and wetsuits for hire and basic tuition for beginners, and most large hotels also have their own watersports clubs.

From Kattavia to Apolakkia ★★

Strong breezes continually buffet the coast west of **Kattavia**, making it increasingly popular with windsurfers prepared to make the lengthy journey.

The road from Kattavia runs out of tarmac just as the coast is reached, but the drive northwards is spectacular until the road cuts inland towards **Apolakkia**. Apolakkia is the largest village in the far south, an agricultural settlement famed for its watermelons. There are tavernas and rooms available for rent which makes the village a good base for local walks, especially since Apolakkia is well served by buses and no car is needed.

Inland from Apolakkia ★★

The gravel track from Apolakkia to Siana (11km; 7 miles) can be walked comfortably in about three hours. Approximately 4km (2½ miles) north of Apolakkia it runs past a reservoir where the valley has been flooded. The **Church of Agios Theotokou** is to the right just before this reservoir and the tiny **Church of Agios Theoros** lies a few hundred metres beyond it. The **Monastery of Agios**

Georgios o Vardos has superb frescoes and is about 3km (2 miles) walk from Apolakkia on a track branching off from the road to the dam.

A road running west to east connects **Apolakkia** with **Gennadi** on the opposite coast. Short detours bring you into hill villages – Arnithea, Istrios, Profilia and Vatio – with their tranquil pace of life. Here the tavernas are used by Greek families.

Mesanagros *

Mesanagros in the centre of the far south can be approached from all directions. The best-surfaced road is from **Lahania** in the east. But for those with the extra protection of a four-wheel-drive vehicle – more for under-body clearance than traction – a more enjoyable option is the route from **Arnithea** over the central spine to **Mesanagros** and then down to Kattavia. Scenically the route is wonderful (and on foot even better). Arnithea village tumbles down a hillside – it has a monastery (**Agios Filemonos**) and a small chapel (**Agios Nectarios**).

Moni Skiadi **

Moni Skiadi, the 13th-century monastery, is situated about 4km (2½ miles) west of Mesanagros. It can be reached on foot from Mesanagros or by car from the west coast. A miraculous icon of the Virgin Mary kept here is one of the best known on Rhodes: at Easter it is carried in procession from village to village and thence to the island of Chalki. A *panayíri* (festival) is held here annually on September 8 to celebrate the birth of the Virgin Mary. The central chapel dates from the 13th century and the build-ings built around it date from the 17th and 18th centuries.

Above: *During the Easter procession, an icon is carried from the monastery at Moni Skiadi through villages to the coast and on to Chalki.*
Opposite: *The reservoir near Apolakkia – a favourite area for walking – blends with the landscape.*

Lindos and the Far South at a Glance

BEST TIMES TO VISIT

Lindos is extremely popular from June–September with package holiday-makers and day visitors: it is also very hot at this time of year. Outside the tourist season Lindos offers a charming escape – the hills around are filled with lovely flowers in spring, and the Easter celebrations here are famous worldwide.

GETTING THERE

Courtesy buses from **Rhodes Diagoras Airport** transport package holiday visitors to their resorts and hotels. Independent travellers can use the public bus service just outside the airport to take them into Rhodes town and back. Lindos is well-served by buses from Rhodes town (a half-hourly service) including the Lindos Express **coach service**. **Buses** for Lindos and the east coast leave **Rhodes town** from **Rimini Square** behind the Nea Agora.

GETTING AROUND

The main square in **Lindos** serves as the bus station. **Afandou** and **Archangelos** are stopping points for all the buses but only some stop at the smaller villages. **Malona** and **Massari** are often stopping points but check the timetable from the tourist office or in **Rodos News**. In the far south bus services are reduced to one per day from Mesanagros to Rhodes

town via Kattavia and along the east coast to Gennadi and Lardos, returning from Rhodes in the afternoon.

WHERE TO STAY

South of Lindos there are numerous hotels, pensions and guesthouses at Pefkos, Gennadi, Lardos, Kiotari and Prasonisi, but many of these are block-booked in high summer by European package holiday companies and all close for the winter months (late October or November to April or May).

Gennadi
LUXURY
Lydian Village, located between Lardos and Gennadi, tel: 22440 47361, fax: 22440 44165. A tastefully designed and furnished complex built around courtyards.

MID-RANGE
Dennis Beach Apartments, tel: 22440 43395. Quiet apartments in the village, nicely furnished and very clean.
Panorama Gennadi, tel: 22440 43315. This is a small, family-run hotel close to the sea.
Betty Apartments, tel: 22440 43020. Furnished apartments to let, with accommodation for up to twelve people.

BUDGET
Panagos, offers studios and a quiet garden in the village.

Kalathos
LUXURY
Lindos Bay, tel: 22440 31501. Imposing hotel with swimming pool, shops and restaurant fronted by its own shingle beach. There is a hotel minibus service into Lindos.

Lardos Bay
LUXURY
Rodos Princess, Kiotari, tel: 22440 47102, fax: 22440 47267. Near the beach 5km (3 miles) north of Gennadi.

MID-RANGE
Kiotari Beach, Asklipio, Lardos Bay, tel: 22440 43251. A small self-contained hotel – rooms have sea views.
Hotel Elioula, tel: 22440 44594. This small hotel (36 rooms), just 300m from the beach, has swimming and paddling pools, snack bars and a TV lounge.

BUDGET
Pension Lindos, tel: 22440 48270. Simple, clean rooms around a pebble courtyard in the centre of the village.

Lindos
LUXURY
Lindos Sun, tel: 22440 48270. Small hotel and bungalow complex.
Lindos Mare, tel: 22440 31130, fax: 22440 31131. Large hotel 2.5km from the village, with restaurant, pool, snack bars, games room and in-house entertainment.

Lindos and the Far South at a Glance

Pefkos
BUDGET
Maria Apartments, tel: 22440 48326, fax: 22440 48127. Recently built apartments with balconies, next to beach, with off-street parking.

Vlicha Bay
LUXURY
Atrium Palace, tel: 22440 31601. A fine hotel offering every facility plus a beach. **Steps of Lindos**, tel: 22440 31062. This is a quiet hotel with a swimming pool and facilities for watersports in the bay. It occupies a commanding position on a hillside overlooking the bay. The sand/shingle beach is a 10-minute walk downhill.

WHERE TO EAT

You will notice that restaurant menus in Lindos are geared to an international clientele although most serve authentic Greek specialities. Many eating places in small towns and villages do not have a specific street address or even a published telephone number. In order to find the recommended restaurant, just ask: locals will know where it is.

Lindos
Agostinos, good 'village' food served with Embonas wines from the barrel.
Dionysos Taverna, excellent Greek food in a rooftop restaurant, and reasonably priced too.

Mavrikos, (main square), superb cooking with an interesting selection of dishes.
Lindian Indian, authentic Indian cooking for those who want something different.
Broccolino, Italian restaurant and bar with a great view of Lindos Bay, serves fresh pasta and pizza.

Pefkos
Butcher's Grill, paradise for the carnivore – traditional village fare at reasonable prices.
To Spitaki, traditional dishes imaginatively updated and served in the gardens of an old village house.
Greek House, for tasty, authentic Greek cooking – both meat and fish dishes are available here.

Gennadi
Memories (close to beach) – a justifiably popular eating place, where fresh fish is imaginatively cooked.
Shanghai Chinese Restaurant, standard Chinese menu; a favourite with visitors looking for a change in diet.

Prasonisi
There are two new budget restaurants at Prasonisi. The recently-built **Lighthouse Taverna** and **Oasis Taverna**, located next to the beach, both offer good fish and grilled meat dishes. Both also offer rooms and studio apartments for rental.

Lardos
Lardos Garden Taverna (on the village square) offers interesting menus with delicious variations on standard Greek fare.
Maria's Restaurant (village square), good sea food, freshly prepared.
Roula's Taverna, (village square), a great place for tasty grilled meats and crisp Greek salads.

TOURS AND EXCURSIONS

There is a wide variety of excursions advertised at the many travel agents. Shop around until you find what suits you best. Generally entrance to ancient sites is free on Sundays. All sites and museums are closed on Mondays.
Locally made lace and embroidery is an ancient Lindian tradition – items are displayed on the rocks leading to the acropolis and in shops in the village. Brightly painted Lindian plates and pottery are favourites with visitors – the designs have an eastern feel attributable to Persian craftsmen who taught the art to locals in the 16th century.

USEFUL CONTACTS

Lindos Clinic, Odos Acropolis, tel: 22440 31224.
Tourist Information, Main Square, Lindos town, tel: 22440 31428/31227.

6
The Interior

The Interior is a useful umbrella term to embrace all those bits of inland Rhodes – especially in the mountains – lying more than a few kilometres from the coast and reached on roads often rutted and potholed.

Although villages in the mountains are few and far between, centuries of human habitation have left their mark on the land, from vineyards on many of the hillsides to the once forested but now starkly denuded slopes of **Mt Ataviros**.

Cooler temperatures, shade and the scent and soft green of pines are powerful magnets drawing people from resorts in hired cars and on organized trips – especially to **Mt Profitis Ilias** and **Petaloudes**, the famed Valley of the Butterflies. But few stay, preferring to return to the coast where their accommodation is. There are very few hotels, though rooms are often available to let in villages (enquire with the tourist police). Nevertheless, for walkers there are numerous tracks, often through forest – or rather the open wooded Mediterranean equivalent – and dramatic landscape. Rhodes has long been a favourite with naturalists who like to keep away from crowds on the coast. Reliable bus services, generally one trip at the beginning and one at the end of a working day, connect larger villages with coastal resorts and often with Rhodes town itself. A car is best, however, for a thorough exploration.

Daytime temperatures can be several degrees below those on the coast. Night-time temperatures in spring and autumn can come as a surprise after a warm day and it makes sense to pack a pullover.

DON'T MISS

★★★ **Mount Ataviros:** the highest point in Rhodes with a ruined temple and views all the way to Crete.
★★★ **Petaloudes:** Butterfly Valley where thousands of colourful Jersey tiger moths gather on migration.
★★ **Embonas:** the wine-making centre of Rhodes.
★ **Psinthos:** and the mountain villages – a different aspect of life on Rhodes and a refuge from the coast.

Opposite: *The olive tree, mainstay of the economy, cannot survive winters with frost.*

THE NORTH
Petaloudes ★★★

The Valley of the Butterflies is well signposted and can be approached from the east or west coasts of the island. From Faliraki or Afandou on the east coast make for Psinthos and then follow signs for Petaloudes from the village square.

In summer numerous coaches bring visitors to this spot, where they are led down through the cool tree-filled valley to see shady rock surfaces and branches of trees covered with thousands of **moths** – not butterflies. The display is created by a single species of moth: the **Jersey tiger moth** (*Panaxia quadripunctaria*) which gathers in the valley during July and August. The insects are attracted by secretions from a tree – *Liquidamber orientalis* – which grows here: droplets of a fragrant resin (once used in the manufacture of frankincense) are secreted by the tree bark. The moths migrate from all over the island (and possibly from Turkey) but numbers are slowly decreasing. The reason is that, in spite of notices, visitors clap or otherwise disturb the nocturnal insects from their daytime sleep. They take flight under stress, with the result that many now die before being able to mate and lay eggs. The moths have attractive chocolate-and-white patterned forewings which show when they are settled; when disturbed the moths reveal brilliant

Central Rhodes

AEGEAN SEA

Cape Agios Minas
Ancient Kamiros
Ferry to Chalki
Mandrikon
Kastellos (Castle)
Kritinia
Makri
Lakkion
Siana
Istrios
Strongili 496 m
Apolakkia
Arnithea 513 m
Moni Skiai
Mesanagros

Kato Kalamon
PARADISI
Damatria
Fanes
Soroni
Theologos
Maritsa
Kalamon
Petaloudes (Valley of the Butterflies)
Kalavarda
Plati
Moni Kalopeta
Psinthos 480 m
Alogna 362 m
Psinthos
Salakos
Kapion
Profitis Ilias 800 m
Dimilia
Eleousa
Archipolis
Skala Nani
Apollona
Platania
Koutsoutis
Kariona Monastery
MESSOVOUNA Loutani
Epta Piges (Seven Springs)
Embonas
Assouri
Mokkaris
Platanero
Archangelos
Mt Ataviros 1215 m
Artamitou Monastery
Kamiri Monastery
Malona
Profitis Ilias 512 m
Feraklos Castle
Ag. Isidoros Monastery
Masari
Agios Isidoros
Laerma
Haraki
Panayia Atrifenou Monastery
Moni Thari
Kalathos
Ypseni Monastery
Pilonas
Lindos Acropolis
Castle
Kontari
Lardos
Lindos
Asklipio
Pefkos (Pefki)
St Paul's Bay
Vati
Kiotari
Lardos Bay
Cape Mirtias
MEDITERRANEAN SEA
Gennadi
Gennadi Beach
418 m

0   30 km

0   5 miles

orange underwings spotted with black.

Outside the moth-watching season, Petaloudes is a very pleasant place to visit with paths, waterfalls and wooden bridges constructed along its length. The best displays of moths are to be found upstream from the ticket office and associated

Above: *Moni Kalopetra – built in 1782 close to the Valley of the Butterflies.*

car park marking the valley's entrance. Open 08:30 to sunset. In the brief Rhodes autumn another spectacle takes place when the leaves of the Liquidamber turn bright orange-red before falling.

Most visitors on whistle-stop bus tours have little time to explore the valley but there is a pleasant round walk (about 1 hour) to **Panayia Kalopetra** (**Moni Kalopetra**) built in 1782 by Alexander Ypsilantis. The path continues uphill through the Valley of Butterflies to this tranquil white-painted monastery where in the courtyard there are picnic tables and the reward of marvellous views.

Psinthos and the Mountain Villages ★★
In recent years Psinthos has been included on the tourist route for the contrived 'village evening' (where you certainly won't see villagers relaxing) of dancing, drinking and eating. Other hill villages tend to be workaday places where Rhodians live going about their business, or from where they travel down to the coast or into Rhodes town to work. Both **Pastida** and **Maritsa**, easy detours on a trip from the northwest coast to Petaloudes, are pleasant, quiet villages to sit with a coffee or some other leisurely drink at a traditional *kafeneíon*. From Psinthos the 'scenic route' (badly surfaced) leads towards **Mt Profitis Ilias** via the hamlet of **Archipolis**, known for its distinctive 'wedding cake' bell tower – and an all too rare petrol station.

AGIOS SOULAS – ON FOOT

Most visitors to the Monastery of Agios Soulas come by car from Soroni for the festival held in its grounds on 20 July.

There is, however, a dramatic walk from Moni Kalopetra. The butterfly walk from Petaloudes follows the river valley – the return route is along the higher, wider track.

From this latter track another runs uphill to the south and then curves westwards on a forest road to Agios Soulas. The chapel of Agios Georgios just above Agios Soulas is reached after about three hours of walking along ridges with dramatic views to the coast.

Below: *Agios Nikolaos Fountoukli (St Nicholas of the Hazelnut) has superb 14th-century frescoes.*

AROUND PROFITIS ILIAS

Both of Rhodes' high mountains are encircled by roads, enabling visitors to gain superb views of the island. Unlike Mt Ataviros,the summit of Profitis Ilias can be easily reached by car.

Eleousa ★★

Many people visit **Profitis Ilias** by travelling up from the west coast (Soroni) or the east coast (Kolimbia) to the village of Eleousa and then taking the road up to the summit. The delightful 15th-century Byzantine chapel of **Panayia Eleousa** just on the edge of Eleousa has frescoes from the 17th and 18th centuries. The remains of an Italian-built plaza form the lovely village square.

About 3km (2 miles) from Eleousa on the minor road leading to the summit is the pretty church of **Agios Nikolaos Fountoukli** (St Nicholas of the Hazelnut), famous for its 14th-century frescoes and a dome which sits on a stone drum. It originally formed part of a late Byzantine monastery and inscriptions inside show it was dedicated to the memory of three children.

Near the summit of **Mt Profitis Ilias** there is a small settlement and the large twin chalets, Elafos and Elafina (Stag and Doe), of a mountain hotel – currently closed.

A path laid out by the Italians leads from a small chapel dedicated to Elijah (Ilias) around the summit ridge. The summit itself is a military outpost and out of bounds.

Platania to Apollona ★★

An alternative route from Eleousa continues around the southern side of the mountain to Platania and then on to Apollona. **Platania** is tiny but has a picturesque Byzantine church with white-painted walls, dedicated to the **apostles Peter and Paul**; a road heads south from the village to Laerma (see p. 99).

Apollona, just along the road, has a **Museum of Popular Art** (enquire about opening times in the village) and still keeps communal ovens for bread and local dishes which are served in the local restaurant.

Salakos ★★

On the north side of the mountain, Salakos, with its tavernas set around a shady square, makes a pleasant place to stop for a while en route to Profitis Ilias from Kalavarda near the west coast. For longer visits Salakos is also a good walking centre since there is a pension in the village.

MOUNT ATAVIROS AND AROUND
Mount Ataviros ★★★

Mycenaean settlers built a shrine to **Zeus** on Mt Ataviros (1215m; 3986ft) – something they often did on the highest point of an island. Only fragments are left of it now, yet with a little effort it can be rebuilt in the imagination. Ataviros is worth scaling at any time of the year for the views out to the islands off the coast. Legend has it that **Althaimenes**, Minoan founder of Kamiros, used to climb here to view his beloved Crete – visible on a clear day (see p. 59). In spring there is a wealth of bushy flowering herbs (sage, thyme, spurge) on the mountain. The round trip to the summit from **Embonas** and back to the village takes about seven hours – rooms can be found in Embonas, allowing for an early start. The terrain is rough and scrub-filled and it makes sense to walk with a companion in case of problems. Also take a supply of food, water and a hat.

CRABS

Many people associate crabs with the seashore and rock pools and it may come as a surprise to find them living in **mountain streams**. Small freshwater crabs (*Potamon fluviatilis*) are also found at **Petaloudes**. They make short work of any of the tiger moths which fall exhausted into the water, eating the bodies and leaving the severed wings to float on the water surface.

ON FOOT

There is a superb walk east from **Agios Nikolaos Fountoukli** through the mountain forests to Salakos. Just before the track reaches the main road into **Salakos** there is an old cobble track (*kalderími*) on which donkeys carried provisions to the top of the mountain via a series of 'switchback' bends. This is now a popular walk coupled with a circum-summit tour on paths the Italians laid out near the top – these skirt a military barracks on the summit itself.

In Salakos, there is the 14th century chapel of **Kimisis Theotokou** which has a pebble mosaic floor.

MOUNTAIN WALKING

The highest ground on Rhodes occurs along the central spine which falls into three sections running south-west of Rhodes town, along the length of the island.

• **Profitis Ilias** – height 900m (2953ft). Ascent by road or from Salakos on the cobbled donkey path.

• **Mt Ataviros** – height 1215m (3986ft). Ascent from Embonas or Agios Isidoros. Embonas – Ataviros – Agios Isidoros 9km (5½ miles).

• **Mt Akramitis** – height 823m (2700ft). Ascent from Siana on path running northwest from main road, approximately 1km (0.6 miles) southwest of Siana, or from Monolithos. Siana – Akramitis – Monolithos 7.5km (4½ miles).
The ascent of both Mt Akramitis and Mt Ataviros requires strenuous walking.

Embonas ★★

This prosperous village in a depopulated region is dedicated to weaving and the production of wines. Another lucrative industry is the 'Greek evening' to which tour operators bring their clients in droves.

The elevation, land aspect and soil types of the surrounding region create microclimates which are ideal for viticulture of several varieties of grapes. The **Emery Wine Factory** in Embonas is open to visitors and gives tastings of its products. Open Monday–Saturday 09:00–15:20; coach parties tend to visit between 10:00–14:00 on request. If the factory is crowded then Embonas has more than its fair share of tavernas which serve local wines.

Agios Isidoros ★★

On the other side of the mountain, this is a picturesque village set in tiers on the southeast slopes of Mt Ataviros. A clear path zig-zags its way up Mt Ataviros, providing an alternative route to the summit; the energetic can carry on down the other side to Embonas (approximately 6 hours in all). A right turning from the road north out of the village takes you on to the poorly surfaced track towards Laerma, 11km (7 miles) away.

Below: *Mt Profitis Ilias – extensive woods and paths provide plenty of invigorating walks.*

THE CENTRE AND FAR SOUTH
Laerma *

Laerma claims to be at the 'centre' of the island. Only 12km (7½ miles) from Lardos on the east coast, it is most often visited by visitors en route for Moni Thari. The attraction of bright lights and availability of jobs near the coast has resulted in an exodus of the young from mountain villages. Laerma and villages south of Ataviros – Istrios, Profilia, Arnitha and Vatio – show a side of Rhodes very different from the busy coasts. There are cafés and tavernas for refreshment but generally the pace of life is slow and most villagers elderly.

Moni Thari **

This monastery lies a short walk (or drive) from the village of Laerma and is deserted but for the sole remaining monk who stays on to keep it open. The monastery building, dedicated to the Archangel Michael, was completed in the 13th century using parts of a much earlier church – north and south walls are 12th century and there are 9th-century remains in the vicinity, making

Opposite top: *Retsina, a resinated wine, is an acquired taste although the local retsina is very good.*
Below: *Far from the crowds – Profilia is one of the whitewashed mountain villages offering a different side of Rhodes.*

Above: *Rhodes has no permanent rivers – dry beds become torrents after the rain.*

WHAT'S IN A NAME?

Rhodos literally means Rose Island and yet, roses as one usually thinks of them do not grow on Rhodes. Some have suggested that the roses in question are rock roses – the pink and white cistus blooms which appear in spring. Greeks tend to use some words as generic terms, for example 'horta' (grass) is used for all green, wild herbs and the term rose may thus have been a general one making Rhodes the 'Island of flowers'.

Several suggestions have been made about the origin of the name. Did it perhaps come from 'roidon' (a local word for pomegranate) or from the Phoenician word for snake 'erod', a reference to Rhodes being overrun with serpents in ancient times?

it the oldest religious foundation on Rhodes.

The inner walls of apse, nave and even dome are frescoed with scenes from the New Testament, plus a few from the Old Testament. Most painting dates from the 16th and 17th centuries – in some parts there are four layers, the earliest attributable to the 11th century.

Local legends associate the monastery's establishment with a Byzantine princess delivered from torment by the appearance of St Michael in her dream. One version suggests that she was cleansed of an incurable disease and another that she was abandoned here by pirates who had kidnapped her.

A joint festival is held here on May 21 to **Agia Eleni** and **Agios Konstantinos**. Keen hikers can enjoy the walk down from the monastery to **Moni Ypseni** – a modern nunnery with a pleasant courtyard containing a fountain and citrus trees.

To the Far South

From **Laerma**, you can explore the interior of the island further south by taking either the track (driveable with care) to **Asklipio** (see p. 85) or to **Profilia** and **Istrios** and thence to **Apolakkia** (see p. 88).

With the aid of a four-wheel–drive vehicle you can continue to the far south on the high 'spine' of the island from **Arnithea** to **Mesanagros** and **Moni Skiadi** (see p. 89).

The Interior at a Glance

Walkers can enjoy the mountains all year – but it can get surprisingly cold in the winter months (Nov–Mar). In summer the mountains offer a welcome escape from coastal crowds and high temperatures. From Mar to late May the flowers are at their best.

The best way to see the interior is to use the coast roads to travel from Rhodes town and then head off into the hills. Hill villages close to Rhodes town have become satellites and many people commute daily. **Buses** travel between Rhodes town (Platia Rimini depot or Averof Street) and Maritsa, Kalithies and Pastida. Check the bus information booth behind the new market for exact departure times. Archipolis has two departures for Rhodes town daily. From Psinthos there is one departure in the morning and afternoon into Rhodes town. Further south regular bus services are few and far between: connecting with villages along the route. Embonas has one bus daily to Rhodes town departing at 07:00 (west coast road) and returning from Rhodes town at 13:15. From Laerma a bus leaves for Rhodes (east coast road) at the same time and returns at 15:00. The free daily newspaper, *Rodos News*, has all bus timetables, as does the NTOG office in Rhodes town.

Because of the scarcity of village buses the interior is best explored by **hire car** or **motorbike**.

Both apartments and rooms are available in Embonas and Lardos, which make good bases from which to explore the interior. It is worth asking about room availability in tavernas, cafés or souvenir shops in Apollona, Agios Isidoros, Laerma, Asklipio, Messanagros, Psinthos and Salakos. The proprietors might have rooms themselves or friends and family who do.

Apolakkia
Mid-range
Amalia, tel: 22440 61365. This is a small, friendly hotel with 34 beds.

Budget
Scoutas, tel: 22440 61251. A small pension with nine rooms, very basic but spotlessly clean.

Salakos
Budget
Nimfi Pension, tel: 22460 22206. Delightful and friendly pension but only four rooms available.

There are tavernas in virtually all the villages mentioned, which provide traditional Greek food – often meat dishes since

fish has to be brought from the coast. Vegetarian dishes also feature. The villages nearest Rhodes are well served with eating places: Archipolis has several cafés and tavernas. Most **Embonas** tavernas are geared to lunchtime coach trips. **Two Brothers Taverna**, Embonas, tel: 22460 41247. Well worth visiting outside the busy lunch and evening periods for excellent traditional meat dishes.

Emery Wine Factory in Embonas is open from Monday–Friday 09:00–15:20. **Moni Thari**, not always open but available for viewing provided someone is there. **Moni Ipensi**, open on request, with mornings usually a good time. Ascent of **Mt Ataviros** begins from Embonas, permitting a traverse to **Agios Isidoros**. All travel agents offer tours to **Petaloudes** (Butterfly Valley).

Shops in the mountains have olive wood carvings, ceramics, embroidered linen, hand-woven carpets and lace. Look for local produce – honey, olive oil, bottled olives, capers, nuts, cakes and pastries. Emery wines are on sale and available for tasting at the winery in Embonas.

See Rhodes at a Glance (p. 49).

7
Near Neighbours

The influence of successive rulers – Venetian, Ottoman and Italian – has given the Dodecanese their distinctive character and architecture. The name Dodecanese (12 islands) is a misnomer: twelve islands were mentioned in Byzantine times and the name stuck. There are about 16 inhabited islands and several bare rocks.

A number of neighbouring islands can be easily visited, either en route to Rhodes by ferry from Athens (Piraeus) or on a day trip, as part of an island hopping itinerary beginning on Rhodes.

Rhodes is both the administrative and economic centre of the Prefecture but the islands are often considered as two groups: northern and southern Dodecanese centred on **Kos** and **Rhodes** respectively. Kos is second only to Rhodes as a tourist attraction in the Dodecanese. **Chalki** and **Nissiros**, untouched by mass tourism, both offer a complete contrast to Kos yet could not be more different: Chalki is an arid limestone outcrop devoid of any natural water supply while Nissiros, one of the few volcanic islands, is fertile with dark sands and hot springs.

Wild, unspoiled **Karpathos**, the second largest of the Dodecanese islands, has a superb coastline and is a mass of wildflowers in spring; **Symi**, having little water must restrict visitors and, like **Tilos**, has an air of exclusivity.

There are very good inter-island connections in the main season. Proximity to the coast of Turkey makes a day trip there easy – note, that visitors with charter flight tickets cannot stay in Turkey overnight under any circumstances: if they do their return ticket will be invalid.

DON'T MISS

★★★ Nissiros: the volcanic landscape with its beaches and caldera.
★★★ Symi: Chorio, the old town high above Yialos reached by the Kali Strata.
★★★ Karpathos: lonely beaches and the ancient mountain village of Olympos.
★★ Chalki: Emborio, with its tiers of Venetian houses above the harbour.
★ Kos: the Asklepeion, ancient centre of healing.

Opposite: *Symi town and harbour – one of the favourite destinations for boat trips from Rhodes.*

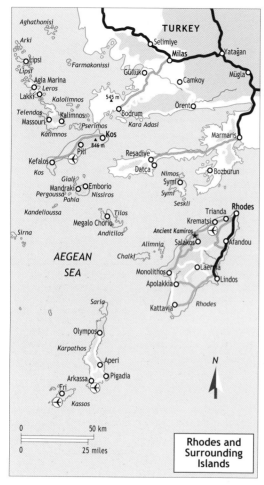

Rhodes and Surrounding Islands

N

CHALKI

Chalki is an intriguing, unspoiled island, friendly and uncompromisingly Greek. The largest of the islands off the west coast of Rhodes, it is a barren rock and its (distinctly 'brackish') water supply comes in tankers from Rhodes. This means that tourist numbers cannot grow too large and the island is perfect for escape and relaxation.

In antiquity copper ore was mined on Chalki (the word *chálkis* means copper) and at the beginning of this century a thriving sponge fishing industry created the island's wealth. When supplies of sea sponges died out in the early 20th century there was mass emigration to Florida. Funds from emigrés built the main road out of the harbour – Boulevard Tarpon Springs (from the name in Florida).

Emborio, the main settlement on Chalki, is the prime focus for daytrippers: its church **Agios Nikolaos** boasts a tall campanile, and a row of ruined windmills stands above the harbour. The village has four tavernas, the same number of bars and a genuine *oúzerie*. Italianate houses built by wealthy sponge fishermen dominate the hillside above the harbour. Many of the old houses have now been restored and painted in

Opposite: *Chalki, a traffic-free island, once thrived on the profits from sponge fishing and now offers escape for the discerning.*

pastel colours – largely as part of a failed venture which was to make the island an international youth centre – and are now available for rent.

Pondamos, reached along the Boulevard Tarpon Springs, has the island's only sandy beach. Nevertheless crystal clear waters around the island make this a snorkeller's paradise. **Yiali**, **Arous** and **Kania** can easily be reached on foot via rough paths – an excursion boat from **Emborio** takes you further afield to **Areta** or **Trachia**.

Chalki is almost traffic-free and ideal for walkers in search of solitude – one walk crosses the stark landscape to the **Monastery of Agios Ioannis Prodhromos** where visitors can stay overnight. **Chorio**, the island's deserted settlement and old town, is closer and now just 5km (3 miles) away via a new road. It comes to life for the festival of the Assumption of the Blessed Virgin Mary held on 15 August each year at the frescoed church of the Panayia. High above **Chorio** there are remains of a fortress built on an ancient acropolis: on a clear day both **Karpathos** and **Crete** are visible on the horizon.

There is a daily ferry link with Rhodes (Kamiros Skala), 10km (6 miles) away, for residents of Chalki, which leaves **Emborio** in the morning and returns to the island in the evening. On Sundays there is a round trip, but otherwise using the ferry means staying on Chalki. In summer there are regular day trips to Chalki from Kamiros Skala: A lack of available rooms can create problems in high season.

If staying on Chalki it is worth taking an excursion by boat to **Alimnia**. This abandoned islet is much greener than Chalki (Chalkians graze their goats there) and has superb beaches.

A ruined fortress is a reminder of past occupation.

THE HUMBLE BATHROOM SPONGE

The industry which made the sponge divers of Chalki and Kalimnos wealthy was hit by 'sponge blight' which decimated the creatures in the early 20th century. Now most sponges for sale on the islands come from the coasts of Sicily and North Africa.

In early times divers descended into the depths on a lifeline weighed down by stones. Later, the invention of diving equipment led to problems as divers suffered from nitrogen narcosis (the bends) from diving too often and resurfacing too quickly.

Right: *Some sponges are still found locally – the bulk is imported, at a price.*

NISSIROS

Nissiros is the only recently active volcanic island in the Dodecanese and its landscape of dark volcanic rocks contrasts with the bare limestone of other islands in the group. The landscape is surprisingly green and lush – volcanic soils are rich in essential minerals and retain water well, even in a dry climate. The island's main income comes from its volcanic heritage – pumice fields and gypsum deposits (especially on **Yiali** just offshore). Nissiros last erupted in 1933: an earlier eruption in 1422 blew off the top of its central peak.

Nissiros lies on a line of volcanoes (including, in past ages, **Aegina**, **Paros**, **Antiparos**, **Milos**, **Santorini** and **Kos**) – the ancients had a different explanation for the island's instability, claiming the angry Titan Polyvotis had been trapped beneath the island by the sea god Poseidon.

Most visitors travel to Nissiros on a day trip which includes the volcanic wastelands in the island's centre. Tickets for organized bus trips to these volcanic areas are sold down on the harbour at Mandraki, but if staying for a few days the local morning bus to the pretty village of **Nikia** allows more time to explore. From the village the walk down into the caldera takes about half an hour, along a path that passes strangely shaped rocks and leads into a desolate area of grey volcanic dust and yellow sulphur deposits. The air is heavy with the smell of hot mud and sulphur – an odour which can cling to your clothes for days after. The biggest of the five craters in the caldera is about 350m (1148ft) wide and 25m (82ft) deep. At **Emborio**, the other village on the caldera rim, there is a Byzantine fort. The village was abandoned after the last eruption but houses are being restored.

Most life centres around **Mandraki**, which serves as both port and capital – a short walk from the harbour takes you to the **Langadaki** district where there is a maze of lanes, many paved with traditional pebble mosaics. Many of the brightly painted houses follow a distinctive design, tall and rather narrow, with balconies.

A fortress – the **Kastro** – stands above Mandraki. It was built by the Knights of St John in 1315. Within the walls is the island's **Historical and Popular Museum** (open daily 10:00–14:30) and a cave with the 15th-century monastery **Church of Panayia Spiliani**. The most famous of the icons in this church is one of the Virgin Mary who appeared to the Crusaders and suggested siting the church in the cave. On the hills above the Kastro lie remains of huge 'Cyclopean' walls of the **Paleokastro**, cut from the volcanic rock and part of the **Dorian acropolis**.

Left: *The lunar landscape of a deep volcanic crater on the island of Nissiros.*

PATMOS

A favourite day trip for holidaymakers – particularly Greeks – is to the island of Patmos. There are day trips from most of the Dodecanese islands, often by hydrofoil.

Patmos is a place of pilgrimage for Christians the world over who visit the **Monastery of St John the Divine**. Boats dock at Skala and it is a short bus or taxi ride (or walk) to the monastery with the village of Chora clinging to the hillside around it. Below the monastery is the cave wherein St John is said to have had the visions which resulted in the Book of Revelations.

Below: *Neo-Classical houses seem to climb the hillside above Yialos harbour on Symi.*

SYMI

The trip from Rhodes to Symi, 24km (15 miles) away, is worth it just for the view of the port of Yialos as the ferry approaches the island. Illuminated tiers of houses piled above the port and the reflection of lights in the harbour water make Symi particularly appealing by night. During the day large numbers of daytrippers from Rhodes fill the lower part of the town and locals and visitors staying on the island tend to 'escape' during the day by walking up to the castle via **Kali Strata** (357 endless steps, if you count), or to island beaches by boat.

A degree of normality returns to Symi after the trip boats depart, leaving yachtsmen of all nationalities enjoying the harbour.

Most of the neo-Classical 'mansions' in **Yialos**, the prime tourist centre, date from the 19th century. The climb up Kali Strata to Chorio takes you back in time surrounded by narrow streets and traditional cubic houses with carved woodwork. There is a 19th-century pharmacy, and the churches of **Agios Panteleimon** and **Agios Giorgios**, as well as a **Museum** with a collection of local finds. Open

Tuesday–Sunday 10:00–14:00. Higher up sits the **Kastro**, where Byzantine walls, built from the earlier Classical settlement were later fortified by the Knights and given the coat of arms of Grand Master d'Aubusson. The acropolis was once the site of a temple dedicated to Aphrodite.

In spring and again in September and October the island is idyllic – July and August brings the crowds and the enclosed nature of the harbour makes it unbearably hot and humid.

In ancient times Symi was famed for the quality of its boat building – its shipwrights built the *Argo* for **Jason and his Argonauts** and this skill was revived under the rule of the Knights; the Turks also used the speedy *skafés* (skiffs) in raids.

Locals grew rich on the profits of a thriving sponge fishing industry and built their mansions in tiers above the harbour. Süleyman saw an advantage in allowing the islanders a measure of independence (and permission to dive in Turkish waters) in return for an annual tribute of the best sponges. The economy floundered, however, with the coming of the steam ship and as a result of the 'sponge blight' of the early 20th century (*see* p. 105). Today the population is but a tenth of what it once was. Imported sponges are still on sale down near the harbour along with local herbs and knick-knacks at a plethora of stalls geared to day trippers.

Walkers will come across numerous tiny churches on Symi (77 in total), many of them near to delightful secluded coves and most of them dedicated to the **Archangel Michael**.

The large and wealthy **Monastery of Taxiarchis Michael Panormitis** (patron saint of sailors), in the south of the island, is popular with daytrippers (boat trips from Rhodes include it with Yialos) and with Greek pilgrims worldwide, especially sailors who invoke the saint's protection with votive offerings of precious metals. Visitors can rent a cell and stay at the monastery if they wish. From the monastery a trail leads through woods to Marathounda Bay – attractive, but not as picturesque as Nanou Bay to the north across the headland.

BEACHES AND ISLANDS

Charani beach is interesting since boat builders working here employ traditional skills. **Pedi Bay**, with fishermans' cottages and a boatyard, is within easy walking distance east of **Yialos harbour**. **Agia Marina** (with a tiny chapel on an offshore islet) is the next beach to the east along the headland. **Agios Nikolaos** with a shingle beach faces **Agia Marina** across the islet. To the west of **Yialos** a coastal path leads to **Nimborio** which has an attractive harbour lined with trees. There are boat trips to offshore islets: **Seskli** and **Strongilos** off the southern tip and **Nimos**, the island at the northern end of Symi.

TILOS

According to Greek mythology, Tilos was named after the youngest son of the sun god Helios and his wife, Alia. The boy came to the island in search of medicinal plants to cure his ailing mother. Tilos' fame in antiquity came from perfume produced here, and also as the birthplace of the poetess Erinna (4th century BC). Under Roman rule the island was largely forgotten but the Knights of St John took over its administration in 1309 and began building a series of seven fortresses.

Somehow, sleepy Tilos has managed to escape the ravages of tourism completely unspoiled. Enthusiastic walkers and birdwatchers have discovered it but kept the secret.

The capital, **Megalo Chorio**, is known to have been inhabited by Minoans and then Mycenaeans. In the 3rd century BC it allied with Rhodes: in 225BC an earthquake destroyed town walls and temples. Today it is a delightful whitewashed village full of colourful flowers in summer. It has a **Venetian Kastro** artfully constructed out of stones from ancient Tilos, incorporating a gateway which once stood on the same site. The pretty church dedicated to the Archangel Michael has icons from an earlier church built inside the Kastro.

Livadia, the port, is the only other inhabited village (there were once nine). It is very popular with Greek families and its tavernas produce good local dishes and bakers make real 'village' bread and cakes. **Livadia** has a long shingle beach with a crystal clear sea. There are several pretty churches close to the waterfront – **Agios Nikolaos**, and further along the road towards the beach, is an early Christian basilica, **Agios Panteleimon**. Around the coast from the port are two more good pebble beaches at **Lethra** and at **Armokosti**.

Mikro Chorio, now uninhabited, is well worth walking to, both for incredible views en route and for its old churches – **Agios Elesas** and **Agios Sotiras** have 15th-century frescoes, while the old church of Timia Zoni has frescoes dating from the 18th century. Below the town there is a long sandy beach at **Eristos**.

In 1971 a ravine near **Mikro Chorio** (the grotto of Hercadio) yielded a wealth of animal bones along with stone-age pottery fragments. The bones were identified as those of deer, tortoises and dwarf elephant (*mastodon*) from the Pleistocene era 10,000 ago when the island became detached from the mainland.

Agios Panteleimon ★★★

One of the best walks on Tilos is the 8km (5 mile) route from Megalo Chorio to the fortified Byzantine **Monastery of Agios Panteleimon** (15th century) built high above the coast. The frescoes within are in poor condition but the view makes the climb worthwhile. From 25–27 July each year the island's biggest festival is held here.

Opposite: *Red pantiled roofs are a feature of many churches on Tilos.*
Below: *Dovecotes are a feature of the landscape on many Dodecanese islands.*

Below: *Greek costumes are retained for traditional festivals on Karpathos, especially in Olympos village.*

KARPATHOS

Karpathos with its wild, rugged landscape is still quiet and unspoiled, even though it boasts a new international airport. With two craggy mountains over 1000m (3281ft) and superb wild flowers, it is a paradise for walkers and naturalists, and the extensive beaches with white sands are often empty.

Many people visit Karpathos on a day trip just to see the village of **Olympos** high in its mountain stronghold. The village can be reached by minibus from the harbour at **Diafani**. In spite of becoming a popular tourist attraction, Diafani is still a treasure house of graceful old buildings with decorated balconies and aged windmills.

From Diafani you can also take a Sunday boat trip to the islet of **Saria**, which forms the northern tip of Karpathos.

The northern part of Karpathos is separated from the south by wild mountainous terrain. A 12km (7½ mile) track which can be traversed by four-wheel-drive vehicle or on foot leads southward from **Olympos** to **Spoa** through dramatic scenery. However, visitors bound for **Pigadia**, the capital, travel instead by caique from Diafani, or visit direct on boats from Rhodes.

Pigadia, the island capital, is an uncompromisingly Greek town situated in **Vrontis Bay** – a one-time pirate cove. It was the site of **ancient Karpathos**, a city dedicated to Poseidon, god of the sea. Vrontis Bay has a good stretch of sand to the north of Pigadia town. There are several hotels, tavernas and some interesting churches including the remains of columns denoting the site of an early Christian basilica named **Agia Fotini**.

The island's main tourist resort is at **Ammopi** around the headland south of Vrontis beach. The series of small bays has become popular with families in recent years. To the north, regular caiques leave Pigadia for the superb beaches of **Kyra Panayia** and **Apella**, set at the foot of dramatic **Mt Kalilimni** (1188m; 3898ft), the highest mountain in the Dodecanese. Myrtonas, to the northwest of Apella beach, holds a popular festival on 22 August.

Arkasa on the west coast is surrounded by fruit groves and has become a thriving tourist centre. A track to the southwest leads to the site of **ancient Arkasa** with Mycenaean ruins (Paleokastro) on the rocky headland. For the explorer there are caves along the coast and remains of early Christian churches with mosaic flooring, such as Agia Sofia and Agia Anastasia. The coast north of Arkasa is rocky and the sea can be rough but there are attractive coves along the coast. One of them, **Finiki**, is a pretty fishing village with a sandy beach. Caiques from here travel to **Kassos** – southernmost of the Dodecanese islands.

A narrow road encircles **Mt Profitis Ilias**, west of Pigadia, passing through mountain villages perched high on hillsides. The route takes in **Menetes**, **Piles**, **Othos**, at 450m (1477ft) the highest village on Karpathos, and **Volada**. Both Menetes and Othos have a craft museum. **Aperi**, the last village before the road returns to Pigadia, was once the capital and still has the reputation of being one of Greece's richest villages, since many expatriates (Americans in particular) have built houses there.

Opposite top: *Some of the most dramatic and rugged terrain in the Dodecanese is to be found on Karpathos.*

A LIVING MUSEUM

Isolation has enabled the village of **Olympos** to remain a repository of ancient traditions and crafts. Bread and delicious vegetable pies are baked in outdoor ovens while two mills in the wonderfully photogenic line of windmills above the village still grind corn for flour. Isolation for centuries has also preserved a unique local dialect with traces of Dorian and Phrygian languages, laws governing female inheritance and traditional melodies played on the *lyra* and *tsamboúna*.

KALIMNOS

Kalimnos can easily be reached by hydrofoil or ferry from Rhodes. This scenically dramatic island is completely unspoiled and rises to 700m (2297ft) on Mt Profitis Ilias at its centre. Its capital, Pothia, is a large Greek town where traditional tavernas and cafés cater for local tastes, but visitors are welcome. Kalimnos still maintains a sponge diving trade although many people have had to leave the island for economic reasons. Islanders claim that the sunsets over Telendos, the islet off its western coast, is the finest in all Greece.

Kos

Kos may be replete with fast food joints and gift shops but can at least guarantee sun, sea and everything for a family holiday at package prices.

The island's important strategic position has meant continuous occupation by successive civilizations from 3500BC. **Minoans** built a settlement where Kos city stands today and they were followed by **Mycenaean** settlers. In Classical times Kos had particularly close links with ancient Halicarnassus (Bodrum in Turkey) and was a member of the six-state alliance, the **Dorian Hexapolis**. Hippocrates, father of medicine, was born on Kos; the **Ptolemies of Egypt** sent their sons to be educated there and the **Romans** valued the island for its production of silk. **Persian** and **Saracen** pirates made frequent raids until the Knights of St John took over in 1315. After the fall of Rhodes to Süleyman in AD1522, the Turks took over in Kos, but by treaty rather than force. Severe earthquakes have bedevilled successive civilizations on Kos, the latest in 1933.

Its central position on ferry routes makes Kos an excellent starting point for island hopping.

Kos Town

In spite of mass tourism much of the charm of Kos town has survived. The **Defterdar Mosque** is still used by the island's small Moslem population and dominates the square, **Platia Eleftherias**. Here you can find the Museum (open Tuesday–Sunday 08:30–15:00) with its imposing 4th-century-BC statue of Hippocrates, the municipal

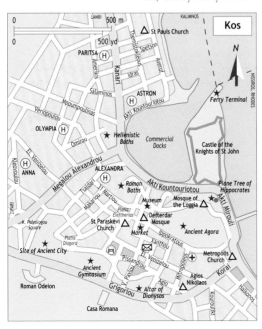

fruit market (Agora) and **Porta tou Forou** (the gate to the ancient Agora).

The **Mosque of the Loggia** (Gazi Hassan Pasha) was built by the Turks in 1786 to overlook the supposedly ancient plane tree with a huge trunk. Hippocrates is said to have taught beneath the tree, but at 500–600 years old it's too young to have shaded the great man himself. The Turks installed a fountain beneath the tree using an ancient sarcophagus as the basin. The **Castle of the Knights** was built from stones of the Agora and was part of a defence system for Rhodes. Grand Master d'Aubusson rebuilt the walls and added extra buildings after an earthquake in 1495. Open Tuesday–Sunday 08:30–15:00.

Roman Finds ★★★

Although foundations of **Minoan** and **Mycenaean** houses have been excavated, it is the Roman remains which are the most revealing of a past lifestyle. Most of the remains lie on either side of Grigoriou Street near the Olympic Airlines office. A lone minaret on the hill now marks the site of the ancient **acropolis**. Across Grigoriou Street the **Roman Odeion** has been restored with its rows of marble seats, and along Tsaldari Street, towards the sea, is the **stadium** with remains of the starting gate and the luxury of a covered running track.

Closest to the Olympic Airlines office itself is the **Altar of Dionysos**, and nearby, hidden in a concrete building, is the **Casa Romana** – a house with mosaics and baths which was destroyed in an earthquake in AD554. Italian archaeologists did a lot of work in the **acropolis** and **forum** just behind the bus station. They also uncovered the main Roman highway – the **cardo** – and houses with mosaics alongside, the **baths** were converted in the fifth century AD to a Christian basilica.

LEROS

In 1989 there was an international outcry at conditions in the mental hospitals on Leros. This publicity served to focus tourist attention on a beautiful, underrated island well worth visiting. Whereas many people were once put off making a day trip to the island, it has since become very popular.

Below: *Tall columns mark the boundary of the Roman Odeion on Kos.*

Below: *Superb Roman mosaics have been discovered on Kos – many are on view in the Archaeological Museum and fortress.*

The Asklepeion ★★★

The Asklepeion in the hills southwest of Kos town was perhaps the most famous centre of healing in the ancient world. It was built some time after the death of **Hippocrates**, though the ruins visible today date from the Hellenistic period when the buildings were reconstructed after an earthquake. Unfortunately, the Knights of St John used the site as a source of cut stone. Zaraphitis, a local antiquarian, rediscovered it in 1902 although his German backer, Herzog, took the credit. The Italians worked on the main reconstruction following the death of Zaraphitis in 1933.

The site is approached via a long avenue of cypress trees and is set on a series of four terraces. At the lowest level are the **Roman Baths** (3rd century AD). On the second level lies the entrance and a spring whose waters were considered to be sacred; on the same level there is a small temple dedicated to **Stertinus Xenophon** who, legend has it, killed the **Emperor Claudius** by choking him with a feather as he slept. Ionic temples to **Apollo** and to **Asklepios** (as well as an altar) stood on the third level, and on the fourth and final level stood the crowning glory: a Doric **Temple to Asklepios** constructed in the 2nd century BC. Open Tuesday–Sunday 08:30–15:00.

Platani *

The **Turkish Quarter** of Kos lies uphill from the centre of town on the way out to the Asklepeion and provides good Turkish food if you cannot afford the outing to Bodrum. The Jewish cemetery lies on the road back into town from Platani – Kos, like Rhodes, had a well integrated Jewish community until German occupation.

Kardamena, the most popular package resort after Kos town, has been developed beyond recognition and should be avoided by anyone who loves Greek islands unless it is to catch a caique to Nissiros or for the walk to the ruined Byzantine fortress. There is a vast Club Med site between **Kamari** and the far southwest of the island, and it's true the local beaches are excellent. At **Agios Stefanos** there is a superb early Christian basilica looking out to the islet of **Kastri**.

Inland lie **Agios Pavlos** and **Agios Ioannis**, two Byzantine basilicas near **Zipari** on the road to **Asfendiou** (a cluster of five villages) set in wooded country. From here a road leads eventually to dramatic **Palaio Pyli**, a deserted Byzantine town perched on a crag. The walls of **Palaio Pyli** were built to merge into natural cliffs – there are several frescoed churches – the oldest dates from the 11th century. Zia, a popular 'tourist village', is also a base for the ascent of **Mt Oromedon**, whose peak **Dikaios Christos** (685m; 2248ft) is the highest on Kos.

Above: *Dramatic sunsets are a feature of many Greek islands – illustrated in Kardamena on Kos.*

BEACHES

The island's beaches have long been a tourist draw: those near town are jam-packed with bodies sizzling in oil. To the south, **Psalidi** (3km; 2 miles) and **Agios Fokas** (8km; 5 miles) are heavily developed; **Embros Therma** (13km; 8 miles) has black sands, thermal springs and fewer visitors.

Both **Kardamena** and **Mastichari** have good beaches but, in season, crowds to match. The coast between **Kamari** and **Agios Stefanos** is dominated by a vast Club Med complex. **Camel** and **Paradise** beaches to the east are very good.

Above: *For a real slice of Turkish life, visit Marmaris on market days.*

TURKEY – MARMARIS, BODRUM

The legendary enmity between Greek and Turk is certainly not apparent when you visit **Marmaris** – nothing gets in the way of good business. If you have flown to Rhodes by charter flight remember the 'Cinderella' clause (no, not glass slippers and home by midnight): stay overnight in Turkey and your ticket is no longer valid. This is to prevent Turkish tourism getting a boost from cheap flights to Greece. No restriction applies to scheduled flights.

Marmaris is a very expensive two hour ferry trip (faster by hydrofoil) from Rhodes: Greek tax is included in the price – Turkish tax is paid on arrival. Passports are given in to the ferry company the day before departure. Most tourist agencies on Rhodes can organize the trip.

Marmaris was reconstructed following an earthquake in 1957 and is now a popular resort with a marina which has approximately 800 berths. Its setting is superb: Marmaris stands in a long bay fringed by pine trees and oleander bushes that burst into pink bloom in summer.

The old quarter is built on the rocky peninsula which surrounds the 16th-century Ottoman citadel. Its winding streets and white houses make a quiet contrast with the busy town centre.

The main shopping area of Marmaris lies in side streets running off **Republic Square** (Cumhuriyet Meydani) and **Atatürk Square**. Salesmen are very persistent but friendly – some carpet sellers could probably sell sand to Arabs after pioneering ice-cream sales to the Inuit. **Bazaar 54** near the marina is a reliable company, and **Silk Road** another which can handle exports with ease.

For a meal look no further than the restaurants around the harbour which provide interesting *mezédhes*.

If you have a scheduled flight and decide to spend a day or more in Turkey there are taxi boats from Marmaris around the coast to the town of **Datça** which sits on a long narrow peninsula. Some boats continue to Knidos, the ancient city at the end of the peninsula – once part of the **Dorian Hexapolis** (with Lindos, Ialyssos, Kamiros, Kos and Halicarnassus) and famed for its wine. For those interested in visiting all these sites, the route **Rhodes–Marmaris–Datça–Bodrum–Kos–Rhodes** making use of local boats is possible though pricey.

Visitors to Rhodes who also intend to include a few days in Kos on their trip can arrange to go to **Bodrum** – the site of ancient **Halicarnassus** where **Mausolus** built his tomb, one of the wonders of the Ancient World, and thereby gave us the word *mausoleum*. The remains lie near the imposing **Medieval Castle of St Peter**. This castle was built by the **Knights of St John** under a succession of Grand Masters, making unsentimental use of the stonework of the ancient city. Bodrum is famous for its **Shipwreck Museum** which displays remains of some of the world's oldest known ships.

MARKET DAY

For those who enjoy markets, the time to visit is on a Friday which is market day in Marmaris – though also the Muslim equivalent of the Sabbath. Find the market and it soon becomes apparent that you are in Asia and not Europe. There is nothing quite like a Turkish market, with stalls selling everything from **fruit** and **vegetables** to **herbs**, **hardware**, '**designer**' label **T-shirts** and **fashion wear** (copyright – what's that?). Marmaris is famous for its **honey**, especially the fragrant variety (*Ãam bali*) made from pine nectar which is sold by street vendors from large jars.

Left: *A multitude of Turkish carpets for sale.*

Near Neighbours at a Glance

BEST TIMES TO VISIT

Smaller islands can be surprisingly crowded from late June to the end of Aug, when they are popular with Greeks and independent travellers as well as package holidaymakers. With few attractions other than beaches, they are dull places when the sun is not shining; go in late May or Jun, or in Sep or Oct. Most hotels, guesthouses and restaurants in the Dodecanese close between Nov and Apr.

GETTING THERE

In summer direct charters serve Rhodes and Kos from major European destinations: charter flights to Karpathos are made from the UK. Other flights to and between islands operated by **Olympic Airlines**: **Kos to Athens** (3 daily), **Rhodes** (3 weekly). Olympic Airlines, tel: 22420 28331. **Karpathos to Athens** (2-3 weekly), **Rhodes** (2-7 daily), **Kassos** (3-5 weekly), **Crete**. Olympic Airlines, tel: 22450 22057. As Rhodes is the administrative centre of the Dodecanese **ferries** connect all the islands in the group, the **Cyclades** and **Piraeus**. In summer the route extends to **Crete** (Iraklion) via **Chalki**, **Karpathos** and **Kassos** (see p. 48).

Rhodes is a good centre for reaching smaller islands in the Dodecanese: regular links to **Tilos**, **Nissiros**, **Astipalea**, **Kos**, **Kalimnos**, **Chalki** and **Karpathos**.

A free daily newspaper, *Rodos News*, has up to date **ferry information**. The NTOG and Tourist Police provide current ferry timetables as will the Port Authority on each island.
Chalki Port Authority, tel: 22460 45220.
Karpathos Port Authority, tel: 22450 22227.
Kassos Port Authority, tel: 22540 41288.
Kos Port Authority, tel: 22420 26594.
Nissiros Port Authority, tel: 22420 31220.
Rhodes Port Authority, tel: 22410 22220.
Symi Port Authority, tel: 22460 71205.

GETTING AROUND

On **Nissiros** there is a regular bus service from the harbour to Pali; buses for Emborio and Nikia leave in the early morning and return mid-afternoon. On **Symi** a handful of taxis and a minibus service connect Gialos with Pedi and Chorio. **Tilos** has a minibus service from Livadia to Megalo Chorio, Agios Antonis and Eristos: many visitors hire mopeds and motorbikes. Several buses per day on **Karpathos** run from Pigadia to Piles (including Aperi, Volada, Othos) and to Ammopi. A daily **boat service** connects Pigadia with Diafani in the north. **Cars** and **bikes** are available for hire. On **Kos** good reliable bus services connect main towns and resorts.

WHERE TO STAY

Most accommodation is pre-booked in peak season. On all islands Tourist Police have lists of rooms. Ask for directions. Locals often meet boats or ferries and offer rooms for rent.

Chalki (*Emborio*)
LUXURY
The Captain's House, tel: 22460 45201. A delightful mansion with a civilized atmosphere (three rooms only).

MID-RANGE
Hotel Chalki, tel: 22460 45390, fax: 22460 45208. A converted olive processing plant with sun terrace.
Nick's Taverna, Pondamos beach, tel: 22460 57248. Rooms with very good food.

BUDGET
Pension Argyrenia. Chalets in quiet garden near beach.

Nissiros
MID-RANGE
Miramare Apartments, near Palia, tel: 22420 31100, fax: 22420 31254. Sea views.

BUDGET
Xenon Hotel, Mandraki harbour, tel: 22420 31011. Cheap and cheerful, handy for ferry.

Symi (*Yialos*)
LUXURY
The Dorian, tel: 22460 71181. Another lovingly restored Captain's House with nine rooms. Expensive but superb.

Near Neighbours at a Glance

Hotel Aliki, tel/fax: 22460 71665. Beautifully restored Captain's House with antique furnished rooms (28 beds).

MID-RANGE
Opera House, tel: 22460 71856, fax: 22460 72034. Peaceful, well-kept apartments in a quiet part of the village.

BUDGET
Taxiarchis, Ano Horio, tel: 22460 72012, fax: 22460 72013. Pretty apartments with terraces overlooking the sea.

Tilos (*Livadia*)
LUXURY
Olympus Apartments, above Livadia, tel: 22460 44365. Self-contained, well-appointed apartments with superb views.

MID-RANGE
Marina Rooms, tel: 22460 44023, fax: 22460 44169. Rooms with balconies, great views of the gulf and village.

BUDGET
Pension Anna, tel: 22460 44334. Just outside Livadia. Peaceful, friendly, clean.

Karpathos
LUXURY
Possirama Hotel, Affoti beach, Pigadia, tel: 22450 22916, fax: 22450 22919. Well-equipped self-catering apartments with balconies (open April–October).
Albatros, tel: 22450 81045. Ammopi beach. Bungalows

close to the beach.
Pension Romantica, Pigadia, tel: 22450 22461. Pension in its own citrus orchard – can accommodate 28.

MID-RANGE
Chryssiakti Hotel, Diafani, near the quay, tel: 22450 51215. Friendly and comfortable, good restaurant.

Kos
Luxury
Iberostar Hippocrates Hotel, Kos Town, tel: 22420 27640, fax: 22420 23590. An expensive, luxury spa hotel.

MID-RANGE
Afendoulis Hotel, 1 Evripilou, tel: 22420 25321. Very friendly and quiet.

BUDGET
Pension Alex, 9 Irodotou, tel: 22420 28798. Favourite with young travellers.
Kos Camping, tel: 22420 23910. Well-equipped camping site reached by minibus from the ferry.

There is an enormous choice of places to eat in Kos Town and the other resorts, from restaurants serving 'English Breakfast' to pizza and pasta joints, Mexican bars and ersatz Chinese and Indian restaurants. If you want more authentic Greek food, watch where the locals eat. Restaurants worth making a special trip include:

Kos Town
Platanos, Platia Platanou, tel: 22420 28991. Imaginative Mediterranean cuisine next to Herodotus's aged plane tree.
Olympiada, Kleopatras 2, tel: 22420 23031. Classic, stick-to-the-ribs Greek cooking in this town-centre taverna.
Nikolas o Psaras, Averof 21, tel: 22420 23098. Kos's finest *ouzeri* – the Greek equivalent of a tapas bar – serves ouzo and snacks.

Symi
Mylopetra, Gialos, tel: 22460 72333. Classy, expensive and elegant with excellent, imaginative seafood dishes.
To Ellinikon, Gialos, tel: 22460 72455. International cuisine but also one of Greece's best wine cellars, open to visitors.

Enquire at hotels or Tourist Police. Daily excursion boats from Rhodes town to Symi, Turkey (Marmaris) and to Chalki from Kamiros Skala.

Hellenic Tourism Organisation (EOT), Rhodes, tel: 22410 23655, for information on all islands.
Astipalea
Tourist Information Office, tel: 22430 61412.
Kos
Tourist Information Office, tel: 22420 24460; Tourist Police, tel: 22420 22444.

Travel Tips

Tourist Information

The **Hellenic Tourism Organisation** (EOT) produces an excellent range of free maps and brochures for all islands and island groups, and also provides free ferry timetables and hotel listings.

London, 4 Conduit Street, tel: (00 44) 20 7495 9300, fax: (00 44) 20 7287 1369; **Australia and New Zealand**, 51–57 Pitt Street, Sydney, tel: (0061 2) 9241 1663, fax: (0061 2) 9235 2174; **Canada**, 91 Scollard St, 2nd Floor, Toronto, tel: (001 416) 968 2220, fax: (001 416) 968 6533. **Athens**: Amerikis 2, tel: (00 30) 21033 10561; Airport, tel: (00 30) 21035 45101 or (00 30) 21035 30445. **City of Rhodes Information Centre**, Son et Lumière Square, tel: 22410 35495; **Rhodes Tourism Promotion Organisation**, Plotarchou Blessa 3, tel: 22410 74555/6, fax 22410 74558.

Websites for Rhodes and the Dodecanese include:
www.rodosisland.gr
www.helios.gr
www.islandsinblue.gr
www.nightliferodos.gr
EOT's website: www.gnto.gr

The *Rodos News* is a free local newspaper which gives information on bus and ferry timetables as well as restaurant listings and events.

Entry Requirements

From 1995 EU citizens can stay indefinitely; most other visitors (including Australia, Canada, New Zealand and USA) are allowed up to three months (South Africa: two months), no visas required. Children must either hold their own passports or be entered in parental passports. Visa **extensions** or **work permits** can be obtained from the Aliens Bureau, Leforos Alexandras 173, 11522 Athens, tel: (00 30) 21077 05711. **Temporary jobs** including bar and restaurant work are not difficult to find on Rhodes. Graduates hoping to find jobs teaching English will need a TEFL qualification.

Customs

Visitors arriving from EU countries may bring in unlimited quantities of cigarettes, cigars, tobacco, wines and spirits, perfumes and other goods, provided that they are for personal consumption or gifts and are not to be resold. If arriving from non-EU countries allowances are reduced to 250 grams of tobacco (200 cigarettes), 2 litres of wine or 1 litre of alcoholic beverage and 50 grams of perfumes.

Health Requirements

No certificates of vaccination are required for visitors.

Getting There

By Air: Direct scheduled flights operate daily to Athens from London and New York (less frequently from Montreal and Toronto) and, in season, to Rhodes and the larger islands which have international airports (Crete, Corfu, Kos, Lesbos, Mykonos, Skiathos, Zakinthos). Operators to Athens include Olympic, BA, Virgin Atlantic, EasyJet and Air Scotland. GB Airways flies from London to Crete and is so far the only scheduled airline direct to the island from the UK. In summer there are numerous charter flights direct to Rhodes from UK, German and Scandinavian airports. Olympic Airlines operate scheduled internal flights to Rhodes (four per day all year round) from Athens. All international flights to Athens including charter flights arrive and depart from **Elevtherios Venizelos International Airport**. Rhodes airport is situated at Paradisi 16km (10 miles) southwest of Rhodes town. Charter flights are met by coaches working for the tour operators. The choice for independent travellers involves: public bus service, taxi or Olympic Airlines bus (tickets from Olympic desk inside airport) to Olympic Airlines office at 9 Odos Lerou Lochou, Rhodes town. Departures leave from this stop approximately 90 minutes before flight time.

Restrictions on charter flights mean validity for a minimum of three days and maximum of six weeks – you must have an **accommodation voucher** tating name, address of destination even if mythical. Charter passengers can only visit a neighbouring country (Turkey) for a day and **not overnight**, otherwise the ticket is invalidated: Turkish officials will stamp a piece of paper to avoid putting a Turkish stamp in your passport. This applies to a current visit only: there is no problem with previous trips to Turkey.

By Road: Routes by car all centre on Athens. From Athens there are regular car ferries to Rhodes. Buses from many European countries travel to Athens. Passengers transfer to ferries or charter flights to reach Rhodes. Due to strife

Useful Phrases

ENGLISH	GREEK
yes	*né*
no	*ókhi*
hello	*khérete*
how are you?	*ti kánete?*
goodbye	*adio*
please	*parakaló*
thank you	*efkharistó*
sorry/excuse me	*signómi*
how much is?	*póso iné?*
when?	*poté?*
where?	*pou?*
I'd like	*thélo*
open	*aniktó*
closed	*kleistó*
one	*éna*
two	*dhío*
three	*tría*
four	*téssera*
five	*pénte*
six	*éxi*
seven	*eftá*
eight	*okhtó*
nine	*enniá*
ten	*dhéka*

in former Yugoslavia, **buses** from London to Athens go via Italy and the ferry to Greece, taking three days. Contact **Olympic Bus Ltd**, 70 Brunswick Centre, London, WC1 1AE, tel: 020 7837 9141.

By Rail: there are no longer direct trains from London to Athens but you can go through Italy via Paris and Bologna to Brindisi and take the ferry to Patras. **British Rail International**, tel: 0845 748 4950.

By Boat: There are daily **ferries** between Rhodes and Piraeus (or Rafina), tickets available from ferry company offices. If intending to interrupt

a journey you must purchase a ticket for each section of the trip. Rhodes is on a number of ferry routes permitting easy links with Astipalea, Chalki, Crete, Folegandros, Kalimnos, Karpathos, Kassos, Kastelorizo, Kos, Leros, Lipsi, Milos, Nissiros, Paros, Patmos, Sifnos, Symi, Syros, Thira, and Tilos. Connections from Kos allow ferry and hydrofoil links with other island groups and with Chios, Lesbos and Samos as well as northern mainland ports Kavala and Alexandroupolis. **International ferries** also connect with Cyprus (Limassol) and Italy (Venice), allowing visitors to bring their cars from Europe avoiding the journey down to Athens. In general, hydrofoils begin to operate in May, are twice as fast as conventional ferries but double the price. Timetables change annually and the best source of information for all ferry timetables is the **Athens Gazette** (on sale in all bookshops and kiosks in Athens). Details pertaining to island neighbours are given in the relevant 'At a Glance section'.

Clothes: What to Pack

In summer, cotton T-shirts and shorts suffice most of the time. Out of season, evenings can be cool and a pullover (even waterproofs) make sense. In more up-market resorts you might want slightly more elegant clothes for evening but leave the tuxedo at home. Hats, sun glasses and UV protection sun cream are advisable during the day.

Money Matters

Currency: in January 2002 the euro replaced the drachma, with notes in denominations of 5, 10, 20, 50, 100, 200 and 500 euros and coins of 1, 2, 5, 10, 20 and 50 euro cents and 1 and 2 euros.

Currency exchange: other than on the remotest islands there is always some means of changing money in a bank (*trápeza*), post office or shipping agent. Post Offices change cash, travellers cheques and euro-cheques and charge less commission than banks. In major resorts the numbers of ACTs (automatic cash tellers) grow yearly.

Travellers cheques: especially Thomas Cook and American Express are accepted in all banks and post offices (passport needed as ID). Cash transfers are best handled by major banks in Athens or Rhodes.

Credit Cards: allow cash withdrawals at banks and ACTs – **Visa** is handled by Commercial Bank of Greece and **Access/Mastercard** by National Bank of Greece.

Tipping: although a 10–15% service charge is added to restaurant bills, Greeks generally leave change as a tip. Taxi drivers, porters and cleaners welcome a tip – the amount depends on service offered.

VAT: is 6%, 13% or 18%, depending on which services or products are provided.

Accommodation

From June to early September most island hotels are geared to the pre-booked package trade – look for last minute bargains from your local travel agents. Out of season it is easy to find a room – prices are 30% lower than in high season. Prices are government controlled according to category (Deluxe, AA, A, B, C, D and E). By law, these rates have to be displayed in each hotel room.

Many **smaller hotels** close out of season but people are often glad to rent rooms and are open to gentle bargaining. The Tourist Police and NTOG office have lists of accommodation (including pensions) on Rhodes – local people go to the harbour to meet ferries and offer rooms for rent. Greek ladies are house-proud and the accommodation will be simple but spotless.

Youth Hostels: there are none on Rhodes.

Camping: there is now only one campsite on Rhodes near Faliraki (open April–Oct, tel: 22410 85515 or 85358).

Eating Out

Most visitors eat in restaurants (*Estiatoria*) or tavernas. In the latter, diners usually begin with starters (*mezédhes*) and follow with meat and fish courses. Some tavernas specialize in fish (*Psarotaverna*) or grills (*Psistaria*). Greeks eat very late and do not hurry a meal.

Transport

Boat: Inter-island services are operated by ferry and hydrofoil (rough seas can play havoc with hydrofoil schedules). To smaller islands there are caique services and **taxi boats** operate between ports, resorts and other beaches. Always check ferry times with the local port authority and book from the boat's central agency where possible.

Road: bus services on Rhodes are better than on most Greek islands. Most villages and all resorts are accessible from Rhodes town. Bus services operate roughly half hourly from the Nea Agora area. For east coast resorts – Platia Rimini. For west coast resorts – Averof Street. An hourly service operates to inland villages and several times daily to the far south. Throughout the summer there is an express service to Lindos.

CONVERSION CHART		
FROM	**TO**	**MULTIPLY BY**
Millimetres	Inches	0.0394
Metres	Yards	1.0936
Metres	Feet	3.281
Kilometres	Miles	0.6214
Square kilometres	Square miles	0.386
Hectares	Acres	2.471
Litres	Pints	1.760
Kilograms	Pounds	2.205
Tonnes	Tons	0.984
To convert Celsius to Fahrenheit: x 9 ÷ 5 + 32		

Many public holidays centre around religious events and precise times depend on the Orthodox calendar:

1 January •
New Year's Day *Protochroniá*
6 January •
Epiphany *Epifánia*
February – March •
'Clean Monday' *Katharí Deftéra* (precedes Shrove Tuesday)
25 March •
Greek Independence Day *Evangelismós*
Late March – April •
Good Friday *Megáli Paraskeví*
Easter Sunday •
Páscha
Easter Monday •
Theftéra tou Páscha
May 1 •
Labour Day *Protomayá*
15 August •
Assumption of the Virgin *Koímsis tis Theotókou*
28 October •
Greek National Day *Ochi Day*
25 December •
Christmas Day *Christoúyena*

Taxis: are a widely used form of transport on all the islands – agree a price before the journey or make sure the meter is running. Sharing is common practice – each person pays full rate for the part of the journey they undertake.
For 24 hour radiocabs, tel: 22410 64712 / 757 / 734.
Cars: charges and fuel costs are high in Greece: the best deals come as part of a 'fly-drive'. For exploring, a car is a useful option but check for any

damage on your vehicle (especially brakes and a spare wheel) before you set out. Check what the insurance covers (usually tyres and under-body damage are excluded). Non–EU citizens need an International Driving Licence. Always pay the supplement for collision-damage waiver to avoid potential problems later. Assistance can be sought via the Automobile and Touring Club of Greece (ELPA) in Rhodes town, tel: 104. If involved in an accident contact the Tourist Police, tel: 22410 27423 (Rhodes), 92219 (Trianda), 51222 (Afandou).
Car hire outlets for Budget, Europe Car, Eurodollar, Avis and Hertz operate at the airports and in Rhodes town.
Motorcycles, Bicycles and Scooters: are a cheap and cheerful way of travelling around. Check the machine carefully first (particularly brakes), wear protective clothing and bring a helmet.

Business Hours

Opening hours vary according to the nature of the business and are confusing even for Greeks. For essentials try between 08:30 and 13:30 – if a shop opens for the afternoon it will be about 16:30–20:00. In popular tourist resorts shops stay open continuously until 22:00.
Banking hours: 08:00–14:00 Monday–Friday. Most museums and archaeological sites are closed on Mondays but otherwise open daily (09:00–15:00). At Kamiros and Lindos sites close at 17:00

(19:00 in summer).

Time Difference

Greece is two hours ahead of GMT. Clocks go forward one hour on the last weekend in March and back on the last Sunday in September.

Communications

Post: There are post offices in Rhodes Town, Lindos and larger villages. Stamps (grammatosima) are also sold at kiosks ands in shops.
Telephones: International calls can be made cheaply from offices of OTE, the Greek telecommunications organisation, where you can make a metered or collect call. There are also numerous international phone booths at all resorts. Prepaid phone cards can be bought in shops and at street kiosks.

Electricity

Mains voltage is 220AC supplied @ 50Hz. Plugs are continental 2-pin – universal adaptors fit them. US appliances need converters.

Weights and Measures

The metric system is generally used throughout Rhodes.

Health Precautions

Visitors to the islands should make sure that their tetanus protection is up to date. Don't underestimate the strength of the sun – even short exposures to sensitive skins can leave a child or adult in agony. Use sun hats, sun glasses, a high protection factor sun screen and practice

GOOD READING

- Alibertis, Antoine (1994) *The Samaria Gorge and its Plants,* Iraklion, Crete.
- Buttler, Karl (1991) *Field Guide to the Orchids of Britain and Europe,* Crowood Press
- **Classics** (Penguin Classics)
  Homer *The Odyssey. The Illiad*
  Herodotus *The Histories*
  Pausanias *The Guide to Greece* (2 vols)
  Plutarch *The Age of Alexander, Plutarch on Sparta, The Rise and Fall of Athens*
  Thucydides *History of the Peloponnese War*
  Xenophon *The History of My Times*
- Durrell, Gerald *My Family and other Animals,* Viking/ Penguin
- Durrell, Lawrence (1961) *The Greek Islands,* Viking/ Penguin
- Durrell, Lawrence (1960) *Reflections on a Marine Venus,* Faber and Faber
- Fowles, John (1977) *The Magus,* Cape, London
- Hardy, David A. (1983) *Greek language and Peoples,* BBC Publications
- Kazantzakis, Nikos *Zorba the Greek*
- *Christ Recrucified*
- *The Fratricides*
- *Freedom or Death,* Faber and Faber/ Simon and Schuster
- Levi, Peter (1980) *Atlas of the Greek World,* Phaidon, Oxford
- Renault, Mary (1986) *The Last of the Wine,* Sceptre, London
- Seferis, George (1924–1955) *Collected Poems,* Anvil Press/ Princetown UP
- Seferis, George (1984) *Flowers of Greece,* Papeco, Athens

sensible sunbathing. Excessive olive oil can cause stomach upsets – retsina, coca-cola and fresh parsley (*mitanós*) can all help. Always carry your own toilet paper. Tap water is safe to drink – bottled water is widely available on Rhodes.

Health Services

There is a reciprocal agreement giving free medical treatment to EU residents. As of 31 Dec 2005 the European E111 form has been replaced by the European Health Insurance Card (EHIC), entitling EU citizens to reduced cost or free medical treatment in Greece and other European Economic Area (EEA) countries. The EHIC is valid for three to five years and covvers any state-provided medical treatment that becomes necessary during your trip. In Greece, state provision is minimal, and the EHIC should not be considered a cut-price alternative to private medical insurance. Make sure your **travel insurance** covers the cost of repatriation in case of medical emergency and offers aeromedical ('medevac') evacuation cover.

Personal Safety

Theft is still not commonplace on Rhodes although it has increased in recent years. Generally harassment of lone females is low-key outside tourist resorts and many women explore the island alone – a sharp *afístime* (leave me alone) or *fíyete* (go away) usually suffices. Greek friends might equip you with a few more forceful phrases. Much has been made in the western press about incidents of rape – they horrify Greeks as much as anyone because the crime is very rare within their society.

Emergencies

Rhodes General Hospital, tel: 22410 22222.
Tourist Police, tel: 22410 27423.
Port Authority, tel: 22410 28888.
Airport, tel: 22410 92981/6.

Etiquette

When visiting monasteries, men should wear long trousers and a shirt (no singlets); women should cover bare`arms and legs to below the knee. Elsewhere, Rhodes is very informal.

Language

Greek is their everyday language, but many Rhodians have a good grasp of English, German, Italian and other European languages. Road signs, shop signs, menus and bus and ferry destination boards and timetables are almost universally in both Greek and English.

INDEX